KIDS STUFF
GERMAN

KIDS STUFF
GERMAN

Easy German Phrases to Teach Your Kids (and Yourself)

Therese Slevin Pirz and Mark Hobson

BILINGUAL KIDS SERIES

CHOU CHOU PRESS
P.O. BOX 152
SHOREHAM, N.Y. 11786
www.bilingualkids.com

Printed in the United States of America

First Edition.
Library of Congress Catalog No. 99-94906

ISBN   0-9606140-4-4

Order direct from the publisher:

Chou-Chou Press
P.O. Box 152
Shoreham, N.Y. 11786
www.bilingualkids.com

To Christine
for whom love, loyalty and honor
are not simply words.
Happy Birthday !

CONTENTS

ACKNOWLEDGMENTS

PREFACE

VOCABULARY

Child's name:_____

Received this book from:_____

Occasion:_____Date:_____

First indication of child's understanding German:_____

_____

Child's first German word:_____

Child's favorite German word:_____

Favorite German books or stories:_____

_____

_____

Favorite German songs:_____

_____

Favorite German movies or videos:_____

_____

_____

Favorite German car:_____

Favorite things to do in German:_____

_____

_____

Favorite German foods:_____

_____

ACKNOWLEDGMENTS

I wish to thank Irmengard Ley and Marie Luise Hobson for their contributions to the text. I hope they are pleased with the results.

My thanks, as always, to my husband, Joe, for his patience and encouragement throughout this project.

PREFACE

This book covers the range of children's interests from infancy to teens. It is meant to cover not so much the calendar age of children, but rather their activities and interests regardless of what birthdays they have passed. This perspective is taken because children develop at different rates. It is hard to predict where they will be in their development and what their experiences will be at any particular age.

The author has researched many books in preparation for the *KIDS STUFF SERIES,* and has found this series to be unique among the vast array of books for children learning foreign languages. The *KIDS STUFF SERIES* translates phrases and sentences to answer the question, "How do you say, '.........................' in German?" Because of this perspective, the user is able to speak *to* children, to carry on a conversation *with* children, and to model sentences that children can use in replying to others.

At whatever age you begin your foreign language adventure, you will find this book to be an invaluable guide for your journey.

Enjoy this book and your children. Good luck and have fun.
Viel Glück!

Scheiden bringt Leiden. Parting is such sweet sorrow.

BEGRÜSSUNGEN   GREETINGS

Start your day and your conversations here. Saying the first few words in German will help you build momentum to continue the rest of the conversation, the rest of the activity, the rest of the day in German. Hearing German spoken will make you feel cheerful especially when it is spoken by you or to you. Hallo!

(Sag,) Hallo!   (Say,) Hello!   *
(Zahk,) HAH-loh!

Hier ist...   The most usual way of
Heer ihst...   answering the telephone
                                       is to say your name:
                                       Here is ...

Ich rufe dich zurück.   I'll call you back.
Ihsh ROOH-feh dihsh TSOO-rewhk.

Wiederhören.   Goodbye. (only on the
VEE-d'r-hehr-e'n.   telephone)

Guten Morgen!   Good morning.
GOO-t'n MOHR-g'n!

13

Guten Tag! Tag!
GOO-t'n tahk! Tahk!

Guten Abend!
GOO-t'n AH-behnt!

Gute Nacht! Bis Morgen!
GOO-teh nakht! Bihs MOHR-g'n!

Es freut mich, dich zu sehen.
Ess froyt mihsh, dihsh tsoo ZAY-'n.

Wie geht's!
Vee gayts!

Wie geht es dir?
Vee gayt ess deer?

(Sehr) gut, danke.
(Zayr) goot, DAHN-keh.

Hast du mich vermisst?
Hahst doo mihsh fehr-MISST?

Lasse dich umarmen!
LAHS-seh dihsh oom-AHR-m'n!

Gib mir einen Kuss!
Ghip meer IGH-n'n kuhss!

Was kann ich für dich tun?
Vahs kahn ihsh fewr dihsh toon?

Wie kann ich dir helfen?
Vee kahn ihsh deer HEHL-f'n?

Nicht so gut.
Nihsht zoh goot.

Good day. Hi!

Good evening. (Greeting).

Good night.
Until tomorrow!

I'm so glad to see you.

How goes it! How do you
do?

How are you?

(Very) well, thanks.

Did you miss me?

Let me give you a hug.

Give me a kiss!   *

What can I do for you?

How may I help you?

Not so good. Not so well.

Es geht mir so-so.
Ess gayt meer zoh-zoh.

Everything is so-so. I'm feeling so-so.

Auf Wiedersehen. Bis nachher!
Aouf VEE-duh-zehn. Bihs nahk-HEHR!

Goodbye. See you later.

Bis bald.
Bihs bahlt.

See you soon.

Viel Spass!
Feel shpahs!

Have a good time!

Winke zum Abschied!
VIHN-keh tsoom AHP-sheet!

Wave good-bye.

Entschuldigung!
Ehnt-SHUHL-dih-gung!

Excuse me.

Wie bitte!
Vee BIT-teh!

What did you say? I beg your pardon!

Alles Gute!
AHL-lehs GOO-teh!

Good luck!

Zum Wohl!
Tsoom vohl!

God bless you! (Sneeze)

Alles Gute zum Geburtstag!
AHL-lehs GOO-teh tsoom geh-BUHRTS-tahk!

Happy Birthday!   *

Frohe Weihnachten!
FROH-eh VIGH-nakh-t'n!

Merry Christmas!   *

Viel Glück im Neuen Jahr!
Feel glewhk im NOY-ehn yahr!

Happy New Year!

Bitte.
BIT-teh.

Please.

15

(Nein), Danke.
(Nighn), DAHN-keh.

(No), thank you.

Nochmals Danke.
NOKH-mahlz DAHN-keh.

Thanks again.

Bitte sehr.
BIT-teh zayr.

You're welcome.

Herzlich willkommen!
HEHRTZ-lihsh vihl-KOHM-m'n!

Welcome!

Sehr angenehm.
Zayr AHN-geh-naym.

Pleased to meet you.

Sprichst du Deutsch?
Shprihkst doo doitch?

Do you speak German?

Ich spreche (nicht) Deutsch.
Ihsh SHPREH-keh (nihsht) doitch.

I (don't) speak German.

Wie heisst du?
Vee highst doo?

What is your name?

Ich heisse ...
Ihsh HIGHS-seh ...

My name is ...
(I am called...)

Wo wohnst du?
Voh vohnst doo?

Where do you live?

Schade, dass du nicht hier bist.
SHAH-deh, dahs doo nihsht heer bihst.

Too bad that you're
not here.

Gruss und Kuss!
Grooss oont kuhss!

Love and kisses.

Ich wünsche dir einen schönen Tag!
Ihsh VEWHN-cheh deer IGH-n'n
SHEWHR-n'n tahk!

I wish you a nice day.
*

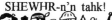

16

Ordnung hat Gott lieb. Cleanliness is next to godliness.

DAS BADEZIMMER   THE BATHROOM

Every family member knows how much time is spent in the bathroom showering, bathing, singing, soaking, admiring... A good time to practice your German looking in the mirror or out loud in the shower.

Musst du zur Toilette gehen?
Muhst doo tsoor twah-LEHT-teh GAY-'n?

Do you need to go to the bathroom?

Sag' mir, wann du zur Toilette gehen musst.
Zahk meer, vahn doo tsoor twah-LEHT-teh GAY-'n muhst.

Tell me when you have to go to the bathroom.

Du hast mir gesagt, dass du zur Toilette gehen musst.
Doo hahst meer geh-ZAHKT, dahs doo tsoor twah-LEHT-teh GAY-'n muhst.

You told me that you had to go to the bathroom

Zieh ab!
Tsee ahp!

Flush the toilet.

17

Klapp den Sitz'runter.
Klapp dain zihts'RUHN-tuh.

Put down the seat.

Wasche dich.
VAH-sheh dihsh.

Get washed.

Dein Gesicht ist schmutzig. Wasche es.
Dighn geh-ZIKHT ihst SHMUHT-tsish.
VAH-sheh ess.

Your face is dirty. Wash it.

Vergiss nicht, deine Hände zu waschen.
Fehr-GHISS nihsht, DIGH-neh HEHN-deh
tsoo VAH-sh'n.

Don't forget to wash your
hands.   *

Hast du deinen Hals gewaschen?
Hahst doo DIGH-n'n hahlz geh-VAH-sh'n?

Did you wash your neck?

Reinige deine Fingernägel.
RIGH-nih-geh DIGH-neh FIHN-guh-nay-gehl.

Clean your fingernails.

Putze dir die Zähne nach dem Essen!
POOT-tseh deer dee TSEHN-eh nakh daim
ESS-'n!

Brush your teeth after eating.

Benutze Zahnseide!
BAY-noot-tseh TSAHN-zigh-deh!

Use floss.

Die Zahnbürste ist auf dem Waschbecken!
Dee TSAHN-bewhr-shteh ihst aouf daim
VASH-bek-'n!

Your toothbrush is on the
sink.   *

Wasche deine Ohren.
VAH-sheh DIGH-neh OH-r'n.

Wash your ears.

Du hast dein Gesicht nicht gewaschen.
Doo hahst dighn geh-ZIKHT nihsht
geh-VAH-sh'n.

You didn't wash your face.

Nun siehst du sauber aus.
Noon zeehst doo ZAOU-b'r aous.

Now you look clean.

18

Dein Gesicht und deine Hände sind sauber.
Dighn geh-ZIKHT oont DIGH-neh HEHN-deh
zihnt ZAOU-b'r.

Your face and hands are
clean.

Du musst ein Bad nehmen.
Doo muhst ighn baht NAY-m'n.

You need to take a bath.

Dreh den Hahn /auf/ zu/.
Dreh dain hahn /aouf/ tsoo/.

Turn the faucet /on/ off/.

Nimmst du /ein Bad/ eine Dusche/?
Nimmst doo /ighn baht/ IGH-neh DOOH-sheh/?

Are you taking a /bath/
shower/?

Ich lasse das Bad für dich ein.
Ihsh LAHS-seh dahs baht fewr dihsh ighn.

I'm running a bath for you.
*

Siehst du das Wasser laufen?
Zeehst doo dahs VAH-suh LAOU-f 'n?

See the water run?

Das Wasser ist /zu heiss / zu kalt/ genau richtig/.
Dahs VAH-suh ihst /tsoo highss/ tsoo kahlt/
gay-NAOU RIHSH-tikh/.

The water is / too hot/ too
cold / just right/.

Lass nicht zuviel Wasser in die Wanne einlaufen.
Lahs nihsht TSOO-feel VAH-suh in dee
VAHN-neh IGHN-laou-f 'n.

Don't fill the tub with
too much water.

Ich wasche dir den Rücken, die Knie und
die Zehen.
Ihsh VAH-sheh deer dain REWHK-'n, dee
k'nee oont dee TSAY-'n.

I'm washing your back,
knees and toes.

Wie du platschen kannst!
Vee doo PLAHT-sh'n kahnst!

How you can splash!

Nimm genug Seife.
Nimm gay-NOOK ZIGH-feh.

Use enough soap.   *

19

Die Seife riecht gut, aber sie ist glitschig.
Dee ZIGH-feh reekht goot, AH-buh zee
ihst GLIHT-shikh.

The soap smells good,
but it is slippery.   *

Du brauchst nicht so viel:
Doo braoukhst nihsht zoh feel:
  Seife, (ZIGH-feh)
  Wasser, (VAH-suh)
  Zahnpasta, (TSAHN-pah-stah)
  Deodorant. (day-OH-doh-rahnt)

You don't need so much:
  soap,
  water,
  toothpaste,
  deodorant.

Trockne dich gut ab, bevor du das
Badezimmer verlässt.
TROKH-neh dihsh goot ahp, buh-FOHR doo
dahs BAH-deh-tsihm-muh FEHR-lehsst.

Dry yourself well before
you leave the bathroom.

Lass das Wasser ab.
Lahs dahs VAH-suh ahp.

Empty the tub.

Mach die Wanne sauber.
Makh dee VAH-neh ZAOU-b'r.

Clean the tub.

Falte das Handtuch.
FAHL-teh dahs HAHN-tukh.

Fold the towel.   *

Gib das Handtuch in die Wäsche.
Ghip dahs HAHN-tukh in dee VESH-eh.

Put the towel in the
laundry.

Hänge das Waschtuch auf.
HEHN-geh dahs VASH-tukh aouf.

Hang up the face cloth.

Hast du das Licht ausgemacht?
Hahst doo dahs lihsht AOUS-gay-makht?

Did you turn off the light?

Möchtest du ein Bad nehmen?
MEHRSH-t'st doo ighn baht NAY-m'n?

Would you like to take
a bath?

Nein. Ich möchte nicht.
Nighn. Ihsh MEHKH-teh nihsht.

No. I don't want to.

20

Das Badezimmer gehört jedem!
Dahs BAH-deh-tsihm-muh geh-HEHRT
YAY-daim!

The bathroom belongs to everybody!

Ich meine, du sollst mit dem
Rasieren beginnen.
Ihsh MIGH-neh, doo zohlst miht
daim RAH-zeer-'n beh-GIHN-n'n.

I think you should start shaving.   *

Wasche später dein Haar!
VAH-sheh SHPEH-tuh dighn HAH-uh!

Wash your hair later!

Du siehst gut aus.
Doo zeehst goot aous.

You look good.

21

Gestriegelt und gebügelt! All spruced up!

SICH ANZIEHEN

GETTING DRESSED

Is it to be the cowboy outfit or the space suit this morning? When you are in a hurry these are not options. Perhaps, instead, when your little girl dresses her dolls or your little guy is playing with his action figures, you and they can try some of these phrases.

Steh auf! Es ist Zeit zum Aufstehen!
Shteh aouf! Ess ihst tsight tsoom
AOUF-shteh-h'n!

Get up! It's time to get up!

Ich wechsle dir die Windeln.
Ihsh VEHK-sleh deer dee VIHN-dehln.

I'm changing your diapers.

Schlüpf mit der Hand durch den Ärmel!
Shlewpf miht dehr hahnt doorkh dain
EHRM-ehl!

Put your hand through the sleeve.

Ich ziehe dir den rechten Schuh an.
Ihsh tsee deer dain REKH-t'n shoo ahn.

I'm putting on your right shoe. *

Du hast den falschen Schuh an.
Doo hahst dain FAHL-sh'n shoo ahn.

You have the wrong shoe on.

Knöpfe dir das Hemd zu!
K'NEHRP-feh deer dahs hehmt tsoo!

Button your shirt!   *

Willst du dir die blaue oder die rote Bluse
anziehen?
Vihlst doo deer dee BLAOU-eh OH-duh dee
ROH-teh BLOO-zeh AHN-tsee-h'n?

Do you want to put on the
blue or the red blouse?

Wo ist dein Hut?
Voh ihst dighn hoot?

Where is your hat?

Mach den Reissverschluss von deiner Jacke zu.
Makh dain RIGHSS-fehr-shlooss fonn
DIGH-nuh YAH-keh tsoo.

Close the zipper on your
jacket.   *

Such nach deinen Handschuhen!
Zookh nakh DIGH-n'n HAHNT-shooh-'n!

Look for your gloves.   *

Vati ist zur Arbeit gegangen. Zieh dich an!
FAH-tee ihst tsoor AHR-bight geh-GAHN-g'n.
TSEE-eh dihsh ahn!

Daddy has gone to work.
Get dressed!

Wir müssen uns anziehen.
Veer MEWHS-s'n oons AHN-tsee-h'n.

We have to get dressed.

Beiss nicht deine Fingernägel!
Bighss nihsht DIGH-neh FIHN-guh-nay-gehl!

Don't bite your nails.

Zieh dir die Unterwäsche und die Hose an!
Tsee deer dee OON-tehr-vay-sheh
oont dee HOH-zeh ahn!

Put on your underpants
and slacks!   *

Trag den neuen Mantel!
Trahk dain NOY-ehn MAHN-tehl!

Wear your new coat.   *

Darf ich dir die Schnürsenkel zubinden?
Dahrf ihsh deer dee SHNEWR-z'n-kehl
TSOO-bihn-d'n?

May I tie your shoe laces? *

23

Du hast einen Knoten in deinem Schnürsenkel.
Doo hahst IGH-n'n k'NOH-t'n in DIGH-n'm
SHNEWR-z'n-kehl.

You have a knot in your
shoe lace.

/Kämm /Bürste/ dir die Haare!
/Kehm/ BEWHR-shteh/ deer dee HAH-reh!

/Comb/ Brush/ your hair!

Die Bürste, der Kamm und die (Fingernagel)
Feile sind auf der Kommode.
Dee BEWHR-steh, dehr kahm oont dee
(FIHN-gehr-nay-gehl) FIGH-leh zihnt
aouf dehr KOHM-moh-deh.

The brush, comb and (nail)
file are on the dresser.   *

Das T-Shirt (aus Baumwolle) wird gut sein.
Dahs TEE-shirt (aous BAOUM-vohl-leh)
veert goot zighn.

The (cotton) T-shirt will
be fine.

Wie gut du aussiehst!
Vee goot doo AOUS-seehst!

How nice you look!

Der Appetit kommt beim Essen. The appetite comes with the eating.

MAHLZEITEN   MEALTIME

Mark the "Beverages," "Desserts," and "Meats," pages of this book in order
to expand your foods vocabulary. You might even want to pretend that you and
your children are one of the birds from the "Birds" page, and select the "Insects"
you might find appetizing. (Something to do AFTER mealtime!) Guten Appetit!

Essen wir!   Let's eat!
ESS-'n veer!

Willst du frühstücken?   Do you want to eat breakfast?
Vihlst doo FREWH-shtewk-'n?

Hör auf zu spielen. Zu Tisch bitte.   Stop playing. Come to the
Hehr aouf tsoo SHPEEHL-e'n. Tsoo   table, please.
tihsh BIT-teh.

Wann gibt es Mittagessen?   When are we having lunch?
Vahn ghipt ess MIHT-tahk-ess'n?

Ich habe /Hunger/ Durst/.   I'm /hungry/ thirsty/.
Ihsh HAH-beh /HOON-guh/ durhst/.

Was möchtest du essen?
Vahs MEHRSH-t'st doo ESS-'n?

What would you like to eat?

Was gibt es zum Abendessen?
Vahs ghipt ess tsoom AH-behnt-ess-'n?

What have we for dinner?

Du hast nichts gegessen.
Doo hahst nihshts geh-GEHS-'n.

You have not eaten anything.

Wann essen wir?
Vahn ESS-'n veer?

When are we eating?

Das Essen ist fertig. Setz' dich.
Dahs ESS-'n ihst FEHR-tikh.
Zehts dihsh.

Dinner is ready. Sit down.

Setz' dich ordentlich hin.
Zehts dihsh OHR-daint-likh hin.

Sit down correctly.

Die Ellbogen gehören nicht auf dem Tisch.
Dee EHL-boh-g'n geh-HEHR-e'n nihsht
aouf daim tihsh.

Your elbows don't
belong on the table.

Möchtest du einen kleinen Snack?
MEHRSH-t'st doo IGH-n'n KLIGH-n'n
shnakh?

Would you like a little
snack?

Willst du Speck oder Kartoffeln?
Vihlst doo shpekh OH-duh kahr-TOHF-fehln?

Do you want bacon or
potatoes?

Greif zu. Nimm noch etwas.
Grighf tsoo. Nimm nokh EHT-vahs.

Help yourself. Take some
more.

Mache dir selbst ein belegtes Brot.
MAH-kheh deer zehlbst ighn beh-LEHK-tehs
broht.

Make yourself a sandwich. *

Darf ich noch Karotten haben?
Dahrf ihsh nokh kahr-ROHT-t'n HAH-b'n?

May I have more carrots?

26

Möchtest du noch mehr? | Would you want more?
MEHRSH-t'st doo nokh mayr?

Ist noch etwas für mich übrig? | Is there any more left for
Ihst nokh EHT-vahs fewr mihsh EWH-brikh? | me?

Ich nehme ein bisschen mehr "cereal." | I'll take a little more
Ihsh NAY-meh ighn BIH-syehn mayr | cereal.
"SEER-i'-uhl".

Ich will nichts mehr. | I don't want any more.
Ihsh vihl nihshts mayr.

Das reicht. (or) Ich bin satt. | I've had enough. (I'm
Dahs righkht.(or) Ihsh bihn sahtt. | full.)

Darf ich mal probieren? | May I have a taste?   *
Dahrf ihsh mahl proh-BEER-'n?

Ich kann nichts mehr essen. | I cannot eat any more.
Ihsh kahn nihshts mayr ESS-'n.

Es gibt nichts mehr. | There is no more.
Ess ghipt nihshts mayr.

Kannst du (mir) bitte das Salz reichen? | Would you pass the salt *
Kahnst doo (meer) BIT-teh dahs zahlts RIGH-k'n? | (to me)?

Gebrauch Gabel, Messer, und Löffel, bitte! | Use your fork, knife, and
Geh-BRAOUKH GAH-behl, MEHS-suh, oont | spoon.
LUHFF-'l, BIT-teh!

Zerdrücke die Banane nicht in deiner Hand. | Don't squeeze the banana
Tser-DREWK-eh dee bah-NAH-neh nihsht | in your hand.   *
in DIGH-nuh hahnt.

Iss den reifen Apfel, aber sei vorsichtig | Eat the ripe apple, but
mit den Kernen. | be careful of the pits.   *
Ihs dain righ-f 'n AHP-fehl, AH-buh
zigh FOHR-zish-tish miht dain KAYR-n'n.

27

Lass mich dein Fleisch schneiden.
Lahs mihsh dighn flighsh SHNIGH-d'n.

Let me cut your meat.

Trinke deine Milch nicht so schnell!
TRIHN-keh DIGH-neh milkh nihsht zoh
shnell!

Don't drink your milk
so fast.

Iss nur ein bisschen! Probier es!
Ihs nuhr ighn BIH-syehn! Proh-BEER ehs!

Eat just a little. Try it.

Das Essen riecht gut.
Dahs ESS-'n reekht goot.

The food smells good.

Schmeckt's?
Shmektz?

Is it good?

Der Kaffee hat einen bitteren Geschmack.
Dehr KAHF-fee haht IGH-n'n BIT-teh-
rehn GHEHSH-makh.

The coffee has a bitter taste.

Der Pudding ist zu /süss /salzig/.
Dehr PUHD-dihng ihst tsoo /sewss/ ZAHL-sikh/.

The pudding is too /sweet/
salty/.   *

Die Sosse ist mild.
Dee SOHS-seh ihst mihlt.

The sauce is bland.

Das Steak ist saftig.
Dahs shtayk ihst ZAHF-tikh.

The steak is juicy.

Magst du den Käse?
Mahgst doo dain KEH-zeh?

Do you like the cheese?   *

Möchtest du ein Schlückchen Tee?
MEHRSH-t'st doo ighn SHLEWKH-k'n tay?

Would you like a sip of tea?

Iss deinen Spinat.
Ihs DIGH-n'n SHPIHN-aht.

Eat your spinach.

Ich mag grüne Bohnen.
Ihsh mahk GREWH-neh BOH-nehn.

I like stringbeans.   *

28

Du kannst dich selbst füttern!
Doo kahnst dihsh zehlbst FEWT-tehrn!

You can feed yourself.

Sprich nicht mit vollem Mund!
Shprikh nihsht miht FOHL-ehm muhnt!

Don't speak with your mouth full.

Giesse die Milch in das Glas!
GEES-seh dee milkh in dahs glahs!

Pour the milk in the glass.

Schneide vorsichtig das Brot!
SHNIGH-deh FOHR-zish-tish dahs broht!

Cut the bread carefully.

Fülle das Glas nicht.
FEHRL-leh dahs glahs nihsht.

Don't fill the glass.

Verschütte das Wasser nicht!
Fehr-SHEWHT-teh dahs VAHS-suh nihsht!

Don't spill the water.

Warum musst du soviel essen?
Vah-ROOM muhst doo zoh-FEEL ESS-'n?

Why must you eat so much?

Iss dein Abendessen auf!
Ihs dighn AH-behnt-ess-'n aouf!

Finish your dinner.

Trink deinen Orangensaft aus!
Trihnk DIGH-n'n ohr-AHN-jen-zahft aous!

Finish your orange juice.

Hast du fertiggegessen?
Hahst doo FEHR-tikh-geh-gehs-'n?

Have you finished eating?

Du hast alles auf deinem Teller gegessen.
Doo hahst AHL-lehs aouf DIGH-n'm TEHL-luh geh-GEHS-'n.

You have eaten everything on your plate.

Guten Appetit!
GOO-t'n ah-peh-TIHT!

Enjoy your meal!

Danke gleichfalls!
DAHN-keh GLIGHKH-fahlz!

The same to you.

29

Das war lecker!   That was delicious!
Dahs vahr LEHK-uh!

Lecker!   Delicious!
LEHK-uh!

So ein leckeres Abendessen!   What a good dinner!
Zoh ighn LEHK-uh-res AH-behnt-ess-'n!

Alles aufgegessen!   All gone!
AHL-lehs AOUF-geh-gehs-'n!

Die Rute macht aus bösen Kindern gute. Spare the rod and spoil the child.

ANWEISUNGEN   DIRECTIONS

These are the pages you use to enlist, explain, persuade, coax, and insist with your child. When all else fails, there is always "Weil ich es sage!" ("Because I say so!") ---appropriate justification in any language.

Was ist das?   What is that?
Vahs ihst dahs?

Es ist ein Pferd.   It's a horse.
Ess ihst ighn fehrt.

Was hörst du?   What do you hear?
Vahs hehrst doo?

So ein Lärm!   What a noise!
Zoh ighn lehrm!

Habe ich dich erschreckt?   Did I frighten you?
HAH-beh ihsh dihsh ehr-SCHREHKT?

31

Was sagst du?
Vahs zahkst doo?

What are you saying?

Was hast du gesagt?
Vahs hahst doo geh-ZAHKT?

What did you say?

Ich höre zu.
Ihsh HEHR-eh tsoo.

I'm listening.

Wie schön du singst.
Vee shehrn doo zinkst.

How beautifully you
sing!   *

Wie gesprächig du bist!
Vee geh-SHPREH-khikh doo bihst!

How talkative you are!

Komm! Setz dich schön (gerade) hin.
Kohm! Zehts dihsh shehrn (geh-RAH-deh) hin.

Come on! Sit up.
(straight)

Setz dich auf meinen Schoss.
Zehts dihsh aouf MIGH-n'n shohss.

Sit on my lap.

Hebe den Kopf.
HEH-beh dain kopf.

Raise your head.

Schau wie stark!
Shaou vee shtark!

Look how strong!

Nimm es (das).
Nimm ess (dahs)

Take it.

Halte die Rassel.
HAHL-teh dee RAHS-sehl.

Hold the rattle.   *

Lass aus!
Lahs aous!

Let go!

Was schaust du dir an?
Vahs shaoust doo deer ahn?

What are you looking at?

Woran denkst du?
Voh-RAHN dehnkst doo?

What are you thinking
about?

Ich kann sehen, dass du träumst.
Ihsh kahn ZAY-h'n, dahs doo trehmst.

I can tell you're dreaming.

Zeig mir wie du deine Arme bewegst!
Tsighk meer vee doo DIGH-neh
ARH-meh beh-VEHKST!

Show me how you move
your arms!

Wer bin ich?
Vehr bihn ihsh?

Who am I?

Wer ist das?
Vehr ihst dahs?

Who is it?

Ich kenne dich.
Ihsh KEH-neh dihsh.

I know you.

Es ist /dein Bruder/ deine Schwester/.
Ess ihst /dighn BROOH-duh/ DIGH-neh
SHVEHS -tuh/.

It's /your brother/ your
sister/.

/Er/ Sie/ ist gross.
/Ehr/ Zee/ ihst grohss.

/He/ She/ is tall.

Es ist /gross/ klein/.
Ess ihst /grohss/ klighn/.

It is large/ small/.

Du hast die Augen von deinem Vater.
Doo hahst dee AOU-g'n fonn
DIGH-n'm FAH-tuh.

You have eyes just like
your daddy's.

Hier ist deine Nase, dein Ohr, dein Mund.
Heer ihst DIGH-neh NAH-zeh, dighn ohr,
dighn muhnt.

Here is your nose, your
ear, your mouth.

Bitte, lächle!
BIT-teh, LEKH-leh!

Please, smile!

33

Ich soll dich fotografieren.
Ihsh zohl dihsh foh-toh-grah-FEER-e'n.

I have to take your picture.
*

Zeig mir ein liebes Lächeln!
Tsighk meer ighn LEE-behs LEHK-ehln!

Show me a nice smile!

Was für eine lange Geschichte!
Vahs fewr IGH-neh LAHN-geh geh-SHIKH-teh!

What a long story!

Das gefällt dir, nicht wahr!
Dahs geh-FELT deer, nihsht vahr!

You like that, don't you!

Lass mich deinen Bauch reiben.
Lahs mihsh, DIGH-n'n baoukh RIGH-b'n.

Let me rub your tummy.

Wohin gehst du?
Voh-HIN gayst doo?

Where are you going?

Steh auf.
Shteh aouf.

Stand up.

Schau...... mal an.
Shaou .... mahl ahn.

Look at.....

Siehst du...?
Zeest doo...?

Do you see...?

Dreh'dich um.
Dreh dihsh uhm.

Turn around.

Kannst du die Maus halten?
Kahnst doo dee maous HAHL-t'n?

Can you hold the mouse?
*

Was hast du im Mund?
Vahs hahst doo im muhnt?

What do you have in your mouth?

Du kannst das nicht in deinen Mund stecken.
Doo kahnst dahs nihsht in DIGH-n'n muhnt SHTEH-k'n.

You cannot put that in your mouth.   *

34

Nicht stossen, spritzen, beissen, weinen!
Nihsht SHTOH-s'n, SHPRIHT-ts'n,
BIGHS-s'n, VIGH-n'n!

No kicking, splashing,
biting, crying!

Stoss mich nicht!
Shtoss mihsh nihsht!

Don't kick me!

Wie du stossen kannst!
Vee doo SHTOH-s'n kahnst!

How you kick!

Du machst mich nass!
Doo makhst mihsh nahs!

You're getting me wet!

Weine nicht.
VIGH-neh nihsht.

Don't cry.

Warum weinst du?
Vah-ROOM vighnst doo?

Why are you crying?

Wo ist die Rassel?
Voh ihst dee RAHS-sehl?

Where is the rattle?

Wo sind die Bauklötze?
Voh zihnt dee BAOU-klehr-tseh?

Where are the blocks?   *

Möchtest du mit dem Ball spielen?
MEHRSH-t'st doo miht daim bahl
SHPEEL-e'n?

Would you like to play
with the ball?   *

Wir gehen die Oma besuchen.
Veer GAY-'n dee OH-mah beh-ZOOK-h'n.

We're going to visit
Grandma.

Wir zeigen ihr, wie gross du bist.
Veer TSIGH-g'n EE-uh, vee grohss doo bihst.

We're going to show her
how big you've grown.

Komm zu Mutti.
Kohm tsoo MUHT-tee.

Come to mommy.

Schau wie du gehst!
Shaou vee doo gayst!

Look how you go! (walk)

35

Lass mal sehen wie du gehen kannst.
Lahs mahl ZAY-'n vee doo GAY-'n kahnst.

Let's see how you walk.

Schau dir die Zähne an!
Shaou deer dee TSEH-neh ahn!

Look at those teeth!

Schmerzen deine Zähne?
SHMEHR-tsehn DIGH-neh TSEH-neh?

Do your teeth hurt?

Nicht so laut!
Nihsht zoh laout!

Not so loud!

Schlag die Trommel!
Shlahk dee TROHM-mehl!

Bang the drum!

Läute die Glocke!
LOI-teh dee GLAH-keh!

Ring the bell!   *

Was für schöne Musik!
Vahs fewr SHEHRN-eh muh-ZIKH!

What beautiful music!

Klatsche! Spiel ein anderes Lied.
KLAHT-sheh! Shpeel ighn AHN-dehr-ehs leet.

Clap!   Play another song.

Hier ist ein Baby so wie du.
Heer ihst ighn BAY-bee zoh vee doo.

Here is a baby like you.

Wer ist das im Spiegel?
Vehr ihst dahs im SHPEE-gehl?

Who is that in the mirror?
                    *

Wo sind / die Füsse / die Augen/ des Babys?
Voh zint/ dee FEWHS-seh/ dee AOU-g'n/
dehs BAY-bees?

Where are/ the feet/
the eyes/ of the baby?

Gehen wir mit dem Kinderwagen spazieren.
GAY- 'n veer miht daim KIHN-duh-vah-g'n
shpah-TSEER-'n.

Let's go for a stroll in your
carriage.

Wir müssen zum Arzt gehen.
Veer MEWHS-s'n tsoom ahrtst GAY- 'n.

We have to go to the doctor.

36

Hab keine Angst. Es ist in Ordnung.
Hahp KIGH-neh ahnkst. Ess ihst in
OHRD-nuhng.

Don't be afraid. It's O.K.

Ich komme! Ich komme, um dich abzuholen!
Ihsh KOHM-meh! Ihsh KOHM-meh, uhm
dihsh AHP-tsoo-hoh-l'n!

I'm coming! I'm coming to
get you!

Jetzt habe ich dich!
Yehtst HAH-beh ihsh dihsh!

Now I've GOT-CHA!

Hast du ......nicht gern?
Hahst doo .....nihsht gehrn?

Don't you like..(something).?

Willst du nicht..... ?
Vihlst doo nihsht.... ?

Don't you want + infinitive?

Willst du /keinen (m)/keine(f)/ kein (n)/ + noun?
Vihlst doo/ KIGH-n'n/ KIGH-neh/ kighn/
+ noun?

Don't you want + noun ?

Lass uns etwas spazieren gehen.
Lahs oons EHT-vahs shpah-TSEER'n
GAY-'n.

Let's take a little walk.

Nimm meine Hand.
Nimm MIGH-neh hahnt.

Take my hand.

Setz dich auf den Stuhl.
Zehts dihsh aouf dain shtoohl.

Sit on your chair.   *

Pass auf die Stufe auf.
Pahs aouf dee SHTOOH-feh aouf.

Watch the step

Steig die Treppe hoch!
Shtighk dee TREHP-peh hokh!

Climb the stairs.   *

Komm vorsichtig die Treppe herunter!
Kohm FOHR-zish-tish dee TREHP-peh
heh-RUHN-tuh!

Come down the stairs.
carefully.

37

Dreh dich nicht (halbwegs) um.
Dreh dihsh nihsht (HAHLP-vehks) uhm.

Don't turn around
(half way).

Steck den Fuss in die Hose.
Shtekh dain fuhss in dee HOH-zeh.

Put your foot in the pants.

Zieh den Arm aus dem Ärmel.
Tsee dain arhm aous daim EHR-mehl.

Pull your arm out of the
sleeve.

Vati zieht dir den Schlafanzug an.
FAH-tee tseeht deer dain
SHLAH-fahn-tsuhk ahn.

Daddy will put on your
pajamas.

Geh und hol deine neuen Schuhe.
Gay oont hohl DIGH-neh NOY-ehn SHOOH-eh.

Go and get your new shoes.

Was hast du in deiner Hand?
Vahs hahst doo in DIGH-nuh hahnt?

What do you have in
your hand?

Gib es mir.
Ghip ess meer.

Give it to me.

Lass /ihn (m) /sie (f) / es (n)/ los.
Lahs /een/ zee/ ess/ lohz.

Let go of it. (m/ f / n)

Fass es nicht an.
Fahs ess nihsht ahn.

Don't touch it.

Geh und hol/ die Bauklötze/ den Ball/.
Gay oont hohl/ dee BAOU-klehr-tseh/ dain bahl/.

Go and get/ the blocks/
the ball/.

Mach es nicht kaputt.
Makh ess nihsht kah-PUHTT.

Don't break it.

Bleib sitzen.
Blighp ZIHT-ts'n.

Stay seated.

Pass gut auf den Teddybär auf.
Pahs goot aouf dain TEHD-dee-behr aouf.

Take good care of your
Teddy bear.   *

Füttere deine Puppe.
FEWT-teh-reh DIGH-neh PUHP-peh.

Feed your doll.   *

Gib /ihm/ ihr/ eine Tasse Tee.
Ghip /eehm/ EE-uh/ IGH-neh TAHS-seh tay.

Give /him/ her/ a cup
of tea.

Streichle den Hund sanft.
SHTRIGHK-leh dain huhnt zahnft.

Pet the dog gently.   *

Hör auf zu /stossen/ schlagen/!
Hehr aouf tsoo /SHTOH-s'n/ SHLAH-g'n/!

Stop /kicking/ hitting/!

Hör auf zu /beissen/ weinen/!
Hehr aouf tsoo /BIGHS-s'n/ VIGH-n'n/!

Stop /biting/ crying/!

Halt!/ Hör damit auf!/
Hahlt!/ Hehr dah-MIHT aouf!/

/Stop! / Stop it!/

Das tut (mir) weh.
Dahs toot (meer) veh.

That hurts (me).

Geh nicht hinein.
Gay nihsht hih-NIGHN.

Don't go in.

Gib mir deine Hand.
Ghip meer DIGH-neh hahnt.

Give me your hand.

Mach nicht zu viel Lärm.
Makh nihsht tsoo feel lehrm.

Don't make too much
noise.

Ruhe, bitte.
ROOH-eh, BIT-teh.

Quiet, please.

Sei still.
Zigh shtihl.

Be quiet.

Ich bin gerade beschäftigt.
Ihsh bihn geh-RAH-deh beh-SHEHF-tikt.

I'm busy now.

Ich bin in Eile.
Ihsh bihn in IGH-leh.

I'm in a hurry.

Ich muss gehen.
Ihsh muhs GAY-'n.

I must go.

Ich komme bald zurück.
Ihsh KOHM-meh bahlt tsooh-REWHK.

I'll come back soon.

Warte! (eine Minute)
VAHR-teh! (IGH-neh mih-NUH-teh)

Wait! (a minute)

Bleib dort!
Blighp dohrt!

Stay there.

Einen Augenblick, bitte.
IGH-n'n AOU-g'n-blikh, BIT-teh.

Just a moment, please.

Beweg dich nicht.
Beh-VEHK dihsh nihsht.

Don't move.

Geh nicht weg.
Gay nihsht vehk.

Don't go away.

Komm weg von dort!
Kohm vehk fonn dohrt!

Come away from there.

Hör auf, das zu tun.
Hehr aouf, dahs tsoo toon.

Stop doing that.

Tu, was ich dir sage.
Too, vahs ihsh deer ZAH-geh.

Do what I tell you!

Tu, wie man dir sagt!
Too, vee mahn deer zahkt!

Do as you are told!

Mach mir keine Schwierigkeiten!
Makh meer KIGH-neh SHVEER-ikh-kigh-t'n!

Don't give me trouble.

Streitet nicht!
SHTRIGH-teht nihsht!

Don't fight!

Wechselt ab!
VEKH-sehlt ahp!

Take turns.

Lass /ihn/ sie/ es/ das/ in Ruhe!
Lahs /een/ zee/ ess/ dahs/ in ROOH-eh!

Don't bother/ him/ her/
it/ that!

Lass die Katze in Ruhe!
Lahs dee KAHT-tseh in ROOH-eh!

Don't bother the cat!　　*

Necke ihn nicht.
NEHK-eh een nihsht.

Don't tease him.

Berühre das nicht. Es ist schmutzig.
Beh-REWH-reh dahs nihsht. Ess ihst
SHMUHT-tsish.

Don't touch that. It's
dirty.

Hebe das nicht auf.
HEH-beh dahs nihsht aouf.

Don't pick that up.

Öffne die Tür.
EHRF-neh dee tewhr.

Open the door.　　　*

Schliess die Tür nicht ab.
Shlees dee tewhr nihsht ahp.

Don't lock the door.

Öffne das Fenster nicht.
EHRF-neh dahs FEHNS-tuh nihsht.

Don't open the window.

Lehne dich nicht zum Fenster hinaus.
LEH-neh dihsh nihsht tsoom FEHNS-tuh
hih-NAOUS.

Don't lean out the window.

Leg die Schachtel dorthin.
Lehk dee SHAKH-tehl dohrt-HIN.

Put the box over there.
　　　　　　　　*

Spring! Spring nicht!
Shpring! Shpring nihsht!

Jump! Don't jump!

41

Langsam!
LAHNG-zahm!

Slowly!

Renne nicht. Geh langsamer.
REHN-neh nihsht. Gay LAHNG-zah-muh.

Don't run. Go slower.

Du stolperst.
Doo SHTOHL-pehrst.

You'll trip.

Beeile dich! Beeile dich nicht.
Beh-IGH-leh dihsh! Beh-IGH-leh dihsh nihsht.

Hurry! Don't hurry.

Wir müssen uns beeilen.
Veer MEWHS-s'n oons beh-IGH-l'n.

We must hurry.

Wir müssen gehen.
Veer MEWHS-s'n GAY-'n.

We must go.

Stelle die Schuhe auf ihren Platz zurück.
SHTEL-leh dee SHOOH-eh aouf EE-rehn
plahts tsoo-REWHK.

Put the shoes back in
their place.   *

Schreib nicht an die Wand!
Shrighp nihsht ahn dee vahnt!

Don't write on the wall.

Tritt zurück!
Triht tsoo-REWHK!

Step back.

Berühre den Herd nicht!
Beh-REWH-reh dain hehrt nihsht!

Don't touch the stove.

Du verbrennst dich!
Doo fehr-BRENNST dihsh!

You will burn yourself.

Hast du dich verbrannt?
Hahst doo dihsh fehr-BRAHNNT?

Did you burn yourself?

Spiel nicht mit Streichhölzern!
Shpeel nihsht miht SHTRIGHSH-herl-tsehrn!

Don't play with matches!
                              *

42

Bleib von der Treppe weg!
Blighp fonn dehr TREHP-peh vehk!

Stay away from the stairs!

Bleib von /dem Grill/ der Strasse/ weg.
Blighp fonn/ daim ghrill/ dehr SHTRAH-seh/
vehk.

Stay away from / the BBQ/
the street/.

Geh nicht über die Strasse!
Gay nihsht EWH-behr dee SHTRAH-seh!

Don't cross the street

Halte dich am Kinderwagen fest!
HAHL-teh dihsh ahm KIHN-duh-vah-g'n
fehst!

Hold onto the carriage.

Schau nach links und nach rechts, bevor du
über die Strasse gehst.
Shaou nakh leenks oont nakh rekhtz,
buh-FOHR doo EWH-behr dee SHTRAH-seh
gayst.

Look left and right before
crossing the street.

Warte, bis die Ampel grün wird.
VAHR-teh, bihs dee AHM-pehl grewhn veert.

Wait for the green   *
traffic light.

Von jetzt an, sei vorsichtig!
Fonn yehtst ahn, zigh FOHR-zish-tish!

From now on, be careful!

Halte es am Griff fest.
HAHL-teh ess ahm grihf fehst.

Hold it by the handle.

Halte es mit zwei Händen.
HAHL-teh ess miht tsvigh HEHN-d'n.

Hold it with two hands.

Beachte was du tust.
Beh-AKH-teh vahs doo toost.

Pay attention to what you
are doing.

Lass es nicht auf den Boden fallen.
Lahs ess nihsht aouf dain BOH-d'n
FAHL-l'n.

Don't drop it on the
ground.

Schneide dich nicht in den Finger! Das
Messer ist scharf!
SHNIGH-deh dihsh nihsht in dain
FIHN-guh! Dahs MEHS-suh ihst scharf!

Don't cut your finger. The
knife is sharp.   *

Fass das nicht an!
Fahs dahs nihsht ahn!

Don't grab that.

Was meinst du?
Vahs mighnst doo?

What do you think?

...,weil ich es sage.
...,vighl ihsh ess ZAH-geh.

...because I say so.

...,weil es halt so ist.
...,vighl ess hahlt zoh ihst.

...because that's the way
it is.

Meinst du...?
Mighnst doo...?

Do you think...?

Bringst du mir bitte den Mop!
Brinkst doo meer BIT-teh dain mohp!

Please bring me the mop.

Kannst du mir mit dem Mittagessen helfen?
Kahnst doo meer miht daim MIHT-tahk-ess-'n
HEHL-f'n?

Can you help me with
lunch?

Kannst du den Teller tragen?
Kahnst doo dain TEHL-luh TRAH-g'n?

Can you carry the dish?

Darf ich dich fragen,...(warum du den
Stein geworfen hast) ?
Dahrf ihsh dihsh FRAH-g'n,...(vah-ROOM
doo dain shtighn geh-VOHR-f'n hahst)?

May I ask you...(why you
threw that stone) ?

Sag deinem Bruder, er soll raufkommen.
Zahk DIGH-n'm BROOH-duh, ehr
zohl RAOUF-kohm-m'n.

Tell your brother to come
upstairs.

44

Sag ihm, er soll kommen.
Zahk eehm, ehr zohl KOHM-m'n.

Tell him he should come.

Deine Schwester soll hereinkommen.
DIGH-neh SHVEHS-tuh zohl
heh-RIGHN-kohm-m'n.

Your sister should come in.

Ich will/ ihn/ sie /sehen.
Ihsh vihl /een/ zee /ZAY-'n.

I want to see/him/ her/.

Du hast dein Hemd schmutzig gemacht.
Doo hahst dighn hehmt SHMUHT-tsish
geh-MAKHT.

You have gotten your shirt
dirty.

Geh in dein Zimmer und zieh dir
ein anderes Hemd an.
Gay in dighn TSIHM-muh oont tsee deer
ighn AHN-dehr-ehs hehmt ahn.

Go to your room and put
on another shirt.

Zeig mir, wo dein Zimmer ist.
Tsighk meer, voh dighn TSIHM-muh ihst.

Show me where your room
is.

Was machst du?
Vahs makhst doo?

What are you doing?

Lass ihn das machen.
Lahs een dahs MAH-kh'n.

Let him do it.

Leg dich hin.
Lehk dihsh hin.

Lie down.

Kannst du das Baby hin und her wiegen?
Kahnst doo dahs BAY-bee hin oont hehr VEE-g'n?

Can you rock the baby?

Setz dich. Bleib sitzen.
Zehts dihsh. Blighp ZIHT-ts'n.

Sit down. Remain seated.

Steh auf. Bleib stehen.
Shteh aouf. Blighp SHTEH-h'n.

Stand up. Keep standing.

45

Hast du das (absichtlich) getan?
Hahst doo dahs (AHP-zikht-likh) geh-TAHN?

Did you do it? (On purpose)

Ich will, dass du mir die Wahrheit sagst.
Ihsh vihl, dahs doo meer dee VAHR-hight
zahkst.

I want you to tell me the
truth.

Bitte, sprich /deutlicher/ langsamer/.
BIT-teh, shprikh /DOIT-likh-uh/
LAHNG-zah-muh/.

Please speak more /clearly/
slowly/.

Hör gut zu!
Hehr goot tsoo!

Listen carefully.

Du bist (heute) /schlechter / guter/ Laune.
Doo bihst (HOI-teh)/ SHLEKH-tuh /
GOO-tuh /LAOU-neh.

You are in a /bad/ good/
mood (today).

Versprichst du, brav zu sein?
Fehr-SHPRIHKST doo, brahf tsoo zighn?

Do you promise to be
good?

Benimm dich!
Beh-NIMM dihsh!

Behave yourself!

Verstehst du, (was ich sage)?
Fehr-SHTAYST doo, (vahs ihsh ZAH-geh)?

Do you understand
(what I'm saying)?

Sei nicht unartig.
Zigh nihsht OON-ahr-tish.

Don't be naughty.

Du bist eigensinnig!
Doo bihst igh-ghen-ZIHN-ikh!

Are you stubborn!

Stell meine Geduld nicht auf die Probe!
Shtell MIGH-neh geh-DUHLT nihsht
aouf dee PROH-beh!

Don't try my patience!

Sei nicht nervös. Beruhige dich.
Zigh nihsht nehr-FEHRS. Beh-ROOH-ih-geh
dihsh.

Don't be nervous.
Calm down.

46

Alles wird schon wieder gut.
AHL-lehs veert shown VEE-duh goot.

Everything will be all right.

Nicht lockerlassen! (or) Nicht aufgeben!
Nihsht LOKH-ehr-lahs-s'n! (or) Nihsht AOUF-gay-b'n!

Don't give up! (or) Don't give in!

Zeig mir, wo es dir weh tut.
Tsighk meer, voh ess deer veh toot.

Show me where it hurts.

Du hast deine Nase angestossen.
Doo hahst DIGH-neh NAH-zeh AHN-gehs-tohs-s'n.

You have bumped your nose.

Reibe es mit der Hand.
RIGH-beh ess miht dehr hahnt.

Rub it with your hand.

Mach den Mund auf!
Makh dain muhnt aouf!

Open your mouth.

Steck den Stein nicht in den Mund.
Shtekh dain shtighn nihsht in dain muhnt.

Don't put the pebble in your mouth.

Mach keine Gesichter!
Makh KIGH-neh geh-ZIKH-tehr!

Don't make faces.

Das tut dir gut
Dahs toot deer goot.

That will do you good.

Putz dir die Nase.
Puts deer dee NAH-zeh.

Wipe your nose.

Atme durch die Nase.
AHT-meh doorkh dee NAH-zeh.

Breathe through your nose.

Sag mir nicht, dass ...
Zahk meer nihsht, dahs...

Don't tell me that...

Lass das Spielzeug mal liegen.
Lahs dahs SHPEEL-tsoik mahl LEE-g'n.

Forget your toy for a moment.

47

Spiel mit deinen eigenen Spielsachen.
Shpeel miht DIGH-n'n IGH-geh-n'n
SHPEEL-zah-k'n.

Play with your own toys.

Vergiss nicht deine Farbstifte (zu bringen).
Fehr-GHISS nihsht DIGH-neh FAHRP-
shtihf-teh (tsoo BRIN-g'n).

Don't forget (to bring)
your crayons.   *

Bring mir...
Brihng meer...

Bring me...

Komm mit mir.
Kohm miht meer.

Come with me.

Sofort!
Zoh-FOHRT!

Immediately!

Geh zur Toilette.
Gay tsoor twah-LEHT-teh.

Go to the bathroom.
(toilet)

Geh zum Badezimmer.
Gay tsoom BAH-deh-tsihm-muh.

Go to the bathroom.
(to wash)

Geh du zuerst!
Gay doo tsoo-EHRST!

You go first.

Hierher! Folge mir!
Heer-HEHR! FOHL-geh meer!

This way! Follow me!

Kannst du es (nicht) selbst machen?
Kahnst doo ess (nihsht) zehlbst MAH-kh'n?

Can('t) you do it yourself?

Geh die Treppe hinauf und hilf Oma.
Gay dee TREHP-peh hih-NAOUF oont
hilf OH-mah.

Go upstairs and help
Grandma.

Spiel /oben (im Haus)/ unten (im Haus)/.
Shpeel /OH-bihn (im haous)/ OON-t'n
(im haous)/.

Play /upstairs/ downstairs/.

Spiel auf dem Bürgersteig!
Shpeel aouf daim BEWR-gehr-shteig!

Play on the sidewalk.

Geh hinaus. Komm herein!
Gay hih-NAOUS. Kohm heh-RIGHN!

Go outdoors. Come
inside.

Schalte das Videogerät ein!
SHAHL-teh dahs FIHD-eh-oh-geh-reht ighn!

Turn on the videocassette
player.

Mach das Licht nicht aus!
Makh dahs lihsht nihsht aous!

Don't turn off the light.

Mach das Licht an!
Makh dahs lihsht ahn!

Turn on the light.   *

Ich kann in der Dunkelheit den Weg nicht
finden!
Ihsh kahn in dehr DOON-kehl-hight dain
vehk nihsht FIHN-d'n!

I can't find the way in the
dark.

Das gehört dir (nicht).
Dahs geh-HEHRT deer (nihsht).

That's (not) yours.

Dieser gehört dir (nicht).
DEE-zuh geh-HEHRT deer (nihsht).

This is (not) yours.(m)

Diese gehört dir (nicht).
DEE-zeh geh-HEHRT deer (nihsht).

This is (not) yours. (f)

Dieses gehört dir (nicht).
DEE-zehs geh-HEHRT deer (nihsht).

This is (not) yours. (n)

Da ist: deiner (m) DIGH-nuh,

There is: yours (m),

  deine (f) DIGH-neh,

  yours (f),

  deins (n) dighns.

  yours (n).

Du darfst im Wohnzimmer nicht essen.
Doo dahrfst im VOHN-tsihm-muh nihsht ESS-'n.

You are not allowed to
eat in the living room.

49

Iss in der Küche,
Ihs in dehr KEWH-kheh,

Eat in the kitchen,

...so dass wir keine Flecken auf den
Teppich bekommen.
...zoh dahs veer KIGH-neh FLEKH-e'n aouf
dain TEHP-pihsh beh-KOHM-m'n.

...so that we don't get
spots on the rug.

Frag mich nicht (wieder)!
Frahk mihsh nihsht (VEE-dehr)!

Don't ask me (again)!

Gib mir /keinen/ keine/ kein/...(m.f.n.)
Ghip meer /KIGH-n'n/ KIGH-neh/ kighn/...

Don't give me...

Warte, bis ich zurückkomme.
Dann sprechen wir.
VAHR-teh, bihs ihsh tsoo-REWHK-kohm-meh.
Dahn SHPREHK-h'n veer.

Wait until I come back.
Then we'll talk.

Tu, was du willst. Du bist /verantwortlich/
zuverlässig/.
Too, vahs doo vihlst. Doo bihst
fehr-AHNT-vohrt-lish /TSOO-fehr-lehs-sish/.

Do what you like. You're
/responsible/ dependable/.

Sei mir nicht ungehorsam!
Zigh meer nihsht OON-geh-hohr-zahm!

Don't disobey me!

Geh zu deinem Zimmer!
Gay tsoo DIGH-n'm TSIHM-muh!

Go to your room.

Streitet euch nicht.
SHTRIGH-t't oish nihsht.

Don't quarrel with one
another.

Mach den Kühlschrank zu.
Makh dain KEWHL-shranhk tsoo.

Close the refrigerator.

Lass dir Zeit.
Lahs deer tsight.

Take your time

50

Vergiss nicht, dir die Füsse abzutreten!
Fehr-GHISS nihsht, deer dee FEWHS-seh
AHP-tsoo-treh-t'n!

Don't forget to wipe your feet.

Geh nicht barfuss draussen!
Gay nihsht BAHR-fuss DRAOU-z'n!

Don't walk barefoot outside.

Was können wir tun?
Vahs KEHRN-n'n veer toon?

What can we do?

Lass uns zusammen versuchen.
Lahs oons tsoo-ZAHM-m'n fehr-ZOOK-h'n.

Let's try together.

Sag mir, was passiert ist.
Zahk meer, vahs pahs-SEERT ihst.

Tell me what happened.

Pass auf, was du hier sagst!
Pahs aouf, vahs doo heer zahkst!

Watch your language!

Du weisst alles besser!
Doo vighst AHL-lehs BEHS-suh!

You have an answer for everything.

Stell das Radio leiser!
Shtell dahs RAH-dee-oh LIGH-zuh!

Lower the radio.

Schalte das Fernsehen aus!
SHAHL-teh dahs FEHRN-zay-'n aous!

Turn off the television.

*

Du darfst dir diese Sendung nicht ansehen!
Doo dahrfst deer DEE-zeh ZEHN-dung nihsht
AHN-zay-'n!

You may not watch this program.

Mach deine Hausaufgaben!
Makh DIGH-neh HAOUS-aouf-gah-b'n!

Do your homework.

Kein Fernsehen, wenn du Hausaufgaben machst!
Kighn FEHRN-zay-'n, vehn doo HAOUS-aouf-
gah-b'n makhst!

No TV when you are doing homework.

51

Hör auf, am Telefon zu sprechen!
Hehr aouf, ahm teh-leh-FOHN tsoo
SHPREHK-h'n!

Stop talking on the phone!

Hör auf mit dem Computer!
Hehr aouf mit dehm kom-PEW-tuh!

Stop using the computer!
                                              *

Es ist zu spät, Freunde einzuladen.
Ess ihst tsoo shpeht, FROIN-deh
IGHN-tsoo-lah-d'n.

It's too late to invite friends.

Dein Buch ist fällig.
Dighn boohk ihst fehl-lish.

Your book is due.   *

Rauchen verboten!
RAUH-k'n fehr-BOH-t'n!

No smoking!

Du hast Training/ Musikunterricht (heute).
Doo hahst TRIGHN-ing/ moo-ZIKH-
oon-tehr-richt (HOI-teh).

You have (sports) practice/
music lessons/ (today).

Leg den Sitzgurt an!
Lehk dain ZIHTS-guhrt ahn!

Put on your seat belt.

Wer vertelefoniert soviel Geld?
Vehr fehr-tehl-eh-fohn-IHRT ZOH-feel
gehlt?

Who's been running up
the phone bill?   *

Du sollst/ den Hund/ die Katze/ füttern!
Doo zohlst/ dain huhnt/ dee KAHT-tseh/
FEWT-tehrn!

You should feed /the
dog/ the cat/.

Du bist dran, mit dem Hund spazierenzugehen.
Doo bihst drahn, miht daim huhnt shpah-TSEE-
rehn-tsoo-gay-'n.

It's your turn to take the
dog for a walk.

Du bist dran, den Müll hinauszutragen.
Doo bihst drahn, dain mewl hee-NAOUS-tsoo-
trah-g'n.

It's your turn to carry out
the garbage.

Zwei Stunden darfst du den Kühlschrank
nicht aufmachen!
Tsvigh SHTUHN-d'n dahrfst doo dain
KEWHL-schrahnk nihsht AOUF-mah-kh'n!

The refrigerator is off limits
for two hours. (For two
hours you may not open
the refrigerator!)

Nimm den Kopfhörer ab!
Nimm dain KOHPF-hehr-uh ahp!

Take off the head set!   *

Komm pünktlich nach Hause!
Kohm PEWNKT-lish nakh HAOU-zeh!

Come home on time!

Komm nicht zu spät!
Kohm nihsht tsoo shpeht!

Don't be late. (Don't come
too late.)

Ich will keine Beschwerden hören!
Ihsh vihl KIGH-neh beh-SHVEHR-d'n
HEHR-'n!

I don't want to hear any
complaints

Das (es) geht.
Dahs (ess) gayt.

That's (It's) all right. It
can be done.

Das (es) geht nicht.
Dahs (ess) gayt nihsht.

Nothing doing! That's
(It's) out of the question!

Lieber nicht.
LEE-buh nihsht.

I'd rather not. Let's not.

53

Viele können mehr denn einer. Many hands make light work.

AUFGABEN *zu* HAUSE   HELPING *at* HOME

Your children are happiest when they are imitating adults in their lives. This includes the work they do. You and your children working together are a natural setting for speaking German together.

Hilf mir den Tisch zu decken!   Help me set the table.
Hilf meer dain tihsh tsoo DEH-k'n!

Du kannst das Tischtuch und die   You can put on the table-
Servietten aufdecken.   cloth and napkins.
Doo kahnst dahs TISH-tukh oont dee
sehr-VYETT-t'n AOUF-deh-k'n.

Decke den Tisch, bitte.   Set the table, please.
DEH-keh dain tihsh, BIT-teh.

Decke den Tisch bitte ab!   Clear the table, please.
DEH-keh dain tihsh BIT-teh ahp!

Hilf mir, das Geschirr /zu spülen/abzutrocknen/.   Help me/ wash/ dry/ the
Hilf meer, dahs geh-SHIHR/ tsoo SHPEW-l'n/   dishes.
AHP-tsoo-trokh-n'n/.

54

Der Spülbecken ist mit Geschirr gefüllt.
Dehr SHPEWL-bekh-'n ihst miht geh-SHIHR
geh-FEWLT.

The sink is filled with
dishes.

Hilf mir das Bett zu machen.
Hilf meer dahs beht tsoo MAH-kh'n.

Help me make the bed.

Hilf mir das Haus zu putzen!
Hilf meer dahs haous tsoo PUHT-ts'n!

Help me clean the house.

Hilf mir die Wäsche zu waschen.
Hilf meer dee VEH-sheh tsoo VAH-sh'n.

Help me do the wash.

Hast du dein Bett gemacht?
Hahst doo dighn beht geh-MAKHT?

Did you make your bed?

Warum nicht?
Vah-ROOM nihsht?

Why not?

(Du bist ein) braves Kind!
(Doo bihst ighn) BRAH-vehs kint!

(You are a) good child!

Du machst mir viel Arbeit!
Doo makhst meer feel ARH-bight!

You make a lot of
work for me!

Mutti kehrt den Fussboden.
MUHT-tee kehrt dain FOOS-boh-d'n.

Mommy's sweeping the
floor.

Vati staubsaugt den Teppich.
FAH-tee SHTAOUP-zaoukt dain TEHP-pihsh.

Daddy is vacuuming the
rug.   *

Der Staubsauger macht ein komisches
Geräusch.
Dehr SHTAOUP-zaou-guhr makht ighn
KOH-misch-ehs geh-ROISCH.

The vacuum cleaner makes
a strange noise.

Was für ein Staub! Stauben wir ab!
Vahs fewr ighn shtaoup! SHTAOU-b'n veer ahp!

What dust! Let's do
some dusting!

Halte das Staubtuch in der Hand
und reibe.
HAHL-teh dahs SHTAOUP-tukh in
dehr hahnt oont RIGH-beh.

Hold the dust cloth in
your hand, and rub.

So ist richtig.
Zoh ihst RIHSH-tihk.

That's right.

Ich nähe einen Rock für dich.
Ihsh NAY-eh IGH-n'n rohk fewr dihsh.

I'm sewing a skirt for you.

Hilf Vati das Mittagessen zu machen.
Hilf FAH-tee dahs MIHT-tahk-ess'n
tsoo MAH-kh'n.

Help Daddy make lunch.

Mutti bäckt einen Kuchen.
MUHT-tee behkt IGH-n'n KOOH-h'n.

Mommy's baking a cake. *

Willst du mir helfen, Plätzchen zu backen?
Vihlst doo meer HEHL-f'n, PLEHTZ-sh'n
tsoo BAHK-'n?

Do you want to help me
bake cookies?

Gib das Mehl dazu.
Ghip dahs mehl dah-TSOO.

Pour in the flour.

Ich schlage die Eier.
Ihsh SHLAH-geh dee IGH-ehr.

I'm beating the eggs.

Ich rühre den Zucker und die Butter schäumig.
Ihsh REWHR-eh dain TSUH-kuh oont dee
BUHT-tuh SHOI-mish.

I'm mixing the sugar
and the butter.   *

Brauchen wir Backpulver?
BRAOU-hk'n veer BAHK-puhl-fuh?

Do we need baking
powder?

Rolle den Teig aus!
ROHL-leh dain tighk aous!

Roll the dough.   *

Wir backen sie im Ofen.
Veer BAHK-'n zee im OH-f'n.

We bake them in the oven.

56

Stelle die Uhr auf eine halbe Stunde!
SHTEL-leh dee OO-uh aouf IGH-neh
HAHL-beh SHTOOHN-deh!

Set the clock for half an
hour.

Die Plätzchen sind fertig!
Dee PLEHTZ-sh'n zihnt FEHR-tikh!

The cookies are done.

Du kannst mir mit dem Bügeln nicht helfen.
Doo kahnst meer miht daim BEWH-gehln
nihsht HEHL-f'n.

You cannot help me iron.

Du kannst mir helfen, die Wäsche zu
sortieren und zusammenzulegen.
Doo kahnst meer HEHL-f'n, dee
VEH-sheh tsoo zohr-TEER-'n oont
tsoo-ZAHM-m'n-tsoo-leh-g'n.

You can help me sort
and fold the laundry.   *

Nach dem Putzen können wir eine
Geschichte lesen.
Nakh daim PUHT-ts'n KERN-n'n veer
IGH-neh geh-SHIHSH-teh LAY-z'n.

After cleaning, we can
read a story.

Bevor du spielst, musst du dein Zimmer
in Ordnung bringen.
Buh-FOHR doo shpeelst, muhst doo dighn
TSIHM-muh in OHRD-nung BRIN-g'n.

Before playing, you must
straighten your room.

Stelle alle Töpfe wieder in den Schrank
zurück!
SHTEL-leh AHL-leh TERP-feh VEE-duh
in dain shrank tsoo-REWHK!

Put all your pots back in
the cabinet.

Willst du mit mir einkaufen gehen?
Vihlst doo miht meer IGHN-kaou-f'n
GAY-'n?

Would you like to go
shopping with me?

Wir wollen etwas zu essen kaufen.
Veer VOHL-l'n EHT-vahs tsoo ESS-'n
KAOU-f'n.

We want to buy something
to eat.

57

Du brauchst neue Kleidung.
Doo braoukhst NOI-eh KLIGH-dung.

You need new clothes.

Hier ist dein Taschengeld.
Heer ihst dighn TAH-sh'n-gehlt.

Here is your allowance.

Kannst du mir helfen, das Geschenk
einzuwickeln?
Kahnst doo meer HEHL-f'n, dahs
geh-SHENK IGHN-tsoo-vihk-k'ln?

Can you help me wrap
the present?

Wir müssen den Schnee schaufeln.
Veer MEWHS-e'n dain shnay SHAOU-f'ln.

We have to shovel the
snow.

Hilf mir den Rasen zu mähen.
Hilf meer dain RAH-z'n tsoo MAY-'n.

Help me mow the lawn.

Säe die Samen in Reihen!
ZEH-eh dee ZAH-m'n in RIGH-h'n!

Plant the seeds in rows.

Es gibt soviel Unkraut.
Ess ghipt zoh-FEEL OON-kraout.

There are so many weeds.

Wir müssen im Garten Unkraut jäten,...
Veer MEWHS-s'n im GAHR-t'n OON-kraout
YEH-t'n,...

We have to weed the
garden...

...damit die Pflanzen wachsen.
...dah-MIHT dee FLAHN-ts'n VAHK-s'n.

...so the plants can grow.

Willst du mir helfen, den Gemüsegarten
zu giessen?
Vihlst doo meer HEHL-f'n, dain
geh-MEWH-zeh-gahr-t'n tsoo GHEE-s'n ?

Will you help me water
the vegetable patch?

Grabe nicht zuviel!
GRAH-beh nihsht TSOO-feel!

Don't dig too much!

Grabe hier im Blumenbeet.
GRAH-beh heer im BLOO-m'n-bayt.

Dig here in the flower bed.

58

Pass auf die Raupen auf!
Pahs aouf dee RAOU-p'n aouf!

Watch out for the
caterpillars!   *

Kannst du die Blätter zusammenrechen?
Kahnst doo dee BLET-t'r tsoo-ZAHM-
m'n-rehk-e'n?

Can you rake the leaves?

Wirf die Blätter /in die Mülltonne/ in den
Müllsack/!
Veerf dee BLET-t'r /in dee MEWL-tohn-eh/
in dain MEWL-zahk/!

Throw the leaves into /the
garbage can/ garbage bag/.

Leg den Gartensprenger /da drüben hin/
hier hin/!
Lehk dain GAHR-t'n-shprehn-guh /dah
DREW-b'n hin/ HEER-hin/!

Put the sprinkler /over there/
here/.

Du kannst die Bäume im Garten beschneiden.
Doo kahnst dee BOY-meh im GAHR-t'n
beh-shnigh-d'n.

You can prune the trees in
the yard.

Es ist zu gefährlich.
Ess ihst tsoo geh-FEHR-lihsh.

It's too dangerous.

Wir bauen einen Karren.
Veer BAOU-'n IGH-n'n KAHR-r'n.

We'll build a wagon.

Kannst du dieses Stück Holz mit Sandpapier
abschleifen?
Kahnst doo DEE-zehs shtewhk holts miht
ZAHND-pah-peer AHP-shligh-f'n?

Can you sand this piece
of wood?

Säge dieses Brett entzwei!
ZEH-geh DEE-zehs brett ent-TSVIGH!

Saw this board in two.   *

Schlage mit dem Hammer auf diesen Nagel!
SHLAH-geh miht daim HAHM-muh aouf
DEE-z'n NAH-g'l!

Hit this nail with the   *
hammer.

59

Willst du zuschauen?   Do you want to watch?
Vihlst doo TSOO-shaou-'n?

Hilf mir am Auto zu arbeiten!   Help me work on the car.
Hilf meer ahm AOU-toh tsoo AHR-bigh-t'n!

/Wasche/ staubsauge/ das Auto.   /Wash/ vacuum/ the car.
/VAH-sheh/ SHTAOUP-zaou-geh/ dahs
AOU-toh.

Kehre den Bürgersteig.   Sweep the sidewalk.
KEH-reh dain BEWHR-gehr-shteig.

Hilf mir den Computer anzuschliessen!   Help me hook up the
Hilf meer dain kom-PEW-tuh   computer.
AHN-tsoo-shlees-s'n!

Erfahrung ist die beste Lehrmeisterin. Experience is the best teacher.

SCHULE zu HAUSE   SCHOOL at HOME

A popular trend is taking place in America where many children and parents are taking charge of their own education. They are doing this at home. For those children who are having classes at home instead of in a school building these sentences will be useful. Of course, these sentences would apply to a classroom situation as well.

Der Schulbus ist gerade vorbeigefahren!
Dehr SHOOL-buhs ihst geh-RAH-deh
fohr-BIGH-geh-fah-r'n!

The school bus just went by!

Es ist Zeit, dass wir (auch) anfangen.
Ess ihst tsight, dahs veer (aoush) AHN-fahn-g'n.

Time for us to start, (too).

Wo haben wir (gestern) aufgehört?
Voh HAH-b'n veer (GUES-tehrn) AOUF-
geh-hehrt?

Where did we stop
(yesterday)?

Es gibt (auch) das Fischprojekt zu machen.
Ess ghipt (aoush) dahs FISH-pro-yekt tsoo
MAH-kh'n.

There's (also) the fish
project to do.

61

Es freut mich, dass wir (heute) zu Hause sind.
Ess froyt mihsh, dahs veer (HOI-teh) tsoo
HAOU-zeh zint.

I'm glad we're home
(today).

Wir werden:
Veer VEHR-d'n:

We will need:

den Tesafilm, eine Heftmaschine,
dain TAY-zah-film, IGH-neh HEFT-
mah-shee-neh,

scotch tape, a stapler,

*

eine Schere, ein Ansteckbrett brauchen.
IGH-neh SHEH-reh, ighn AHN-shtehk-
breht BRAOU-hk'n.

scissors, poster board.

Es gibt keine Heftklammern.
Ess ghipt KIGH-neh HEFT-klahm-mehrn.

There are no staples.

Müssen wir Wissenschaft lernen?
MEWHS-s'n veer VIHS-s'n-shaft LEHRN-'n?

Do we have to do science?

Du kannst ... lesen.
Doo kahnst ... LAY-z'n.

You can read...

...während ich mit deinem Bruder arbeite.
...VEHR-ent ihsh miht DIGH-n'm
BROOH-duh AHR-bigh-teh.

...while I work with your
brother.

Willst du eine Frage stellen?
Vihlst doo IGH-neh FRAH-geh SHTEL-l'n?

Do you want to ask a
question?

Zeige deiner Schwester,
TSIGH-geh DIGH-nuh SHVEHS-tuh,

Show your sister...

...wie man die Matheaufgabe macht.
...vee mahn dee MAH-teh-aouf-gah-beh makht.

...how (one does)   *
to do her math homework.

Mutti, der Locher ist geklemmt!
MUHT-tee, dehr LOH-kuh ihst
geh-KLEMMT!

Mom, the hole punch is
stuck.

62

Machen wir eine Erholungspause!
MAH-kh'n veer IGH-neh ehr-HOH-
lungs-paou-seh!

Wir arbeiten im Garten.
Veer AHR-bigh-t'n im GAHR-t'n.

Wenn wir zurückkommen:
Vehn veer tsoo-REWHK-kohm-m'n:

(dann) lesen wir,
(dahn) LAY-z'n veer,

(dann) gehen wir on-line,
(dahn) GAY-'n veer on-line,

(dann) schicken wir unsrem Vetter ein e-mail,
(dahn) SHICK-e'n veer OONS-rehm FEHT-tehr
ighn e-mail,

(dann) backen wir für Onkel Peter Plätzchen,
(dahn) BAH-k'n veer fewr OHN-kehl Peter
PLETZ-sh'n,

(dann) malen wir ein Bild für Vati.
(dahn) MAH-l'n veer ighn bihlt fewr FAH-tee.

Es freut mich, dass wir keine Prüfungen haben.
Ess froyt mihsh, dahs veer KIGH-neh
PREW-fuhn-g'n HAH-b'n.

Wir müssen lernen. Üben wir!
Veer MEWHS-s'n LEHR-n'n. EWH-behn veer!

Das muss man lernen.
Dahs muhs mahn LEHR-n'n.

Ich brauche mehr Zeit für meine Musik.
Ihsh BRAOU-sheh mayr tsight fewr
MIGH-neh moo-ZEEK.

Let's take a break and relax.
(Let's take a relaxation break.)

We'll work in the garden. *

When we come back:

(then) we'll read,

(then) go on-line,

(then) we'll send our cousin an E-mail,

(then) we'll bake cookies for Uncle Peter,

paint a picture for Daddy.

I'm glad, we don't have any exams.

We have to study.
Let's practice!

You've got to learn that.

I need extra time for *
my music.

63

Darf ich Geschichte überspringen?
Dahrf ihsh geh-SHIKH-teh ewh-buh-
SHPRIN-g'n?

May I skip history?

Meine Farbstifte fehlen.
MIGH-neh FAHRP-shtif-teh FEH-l'n.

My /colored pencils/   *
crayons/are missing.

Hat jemand sie gesehen?
Haht YEH-mahnt zee geh-ZAY-'n?

Has anyone seen them?

Ihr habt sehr viel gearbeitet!
EE-uh hapt zayr feel geh-AHR-bigh-teht!

You (pl) have worked
a lot.

Du hast etwas Nettes verdient!
Doo hahst EHT-vahs NEHT-tehs fehr-DEENT!

You have earned
something nice.   *

Die Aufgabe ist /leicht/ schwer/.
Dee AOUF-gah-beh ihst/ lighkt/ shvehr/.

The lesson is /easy/
difficult/.

Räum alles auf!
Roym AHL-lehs aouf!

Clean everything up!

Wirf die Abfälle in den Papierkorb!
Veerf dee AHP-fehl-leh in dain pah-PEER-
kohrp!

Throw the trash in the
wastebasket.

Tatsachen sind stärker als Worte. Actions speak louder than words.

LOBWORTE   WORDS *of* PRAISE

All the ways to say "You're tops!" "None better!" "Wonderful, Wonderful you!"
and many, many more. Use this chapter *often*. You and your child will LOVE it.

Was für eine schőne Stimme!   What a beautiful voice!
Vahs fewr IGH-neh SHEHR-neh SHTIHM-meh!

Du /gehst/ zeichnest/ sprichst/ singst/ tanzt/ gut.   You /walk/ draw/ speak/
Doo /gayst/TSIGHKH-nehst/ shprihkhst/ zinkst/   sing/ dance/ well.
tahnst/ goot.

Wie gut du /isst/ schreibst/ schwimmst/ spielst/!   How well/you eat/ write /
Vee goot doo /ihst/ shrighpst/ shvimmst/ shpeelst/!   swim / play/.

Du bist prima. Du bist ein Genie!   You're wonderful. You're
Doo bihst PREE-mah. Doo bihst ighn   a genius.
zhay-NEE!

Wie/ nett/ hübsch/du bist!   How /nice/ cute/ you are.
Vee /nehtt/ hewbsh/ doo bihst!

65

Wie/ gutaussehend/ stark/ du bist!
Vee/ goot-AOUS-zeh-ehnt/ shtahrk/ doo bihst!

How/handsome/ strong/ you are.

Wie tapfer du bist!
Vee TAP-fehr doo bihst!

How brave you are.

Dieses Kleid passt dir gut.
DEE-zehs klight pahst deer goot.

This dress suits you well.

Was für schöne Augen du hast!
Vahs fewr SHEHR-neh AOU-g'n doo hahst!

What pretty eyes you have.

Ich habe/ deine Augen/ deine Hände/ deinen
Bauch/sehr gern.
Ihsh HAH-beh/ DIGH-neh AOU-g'n/ DIGH-neh
HEHN-deh/ DIGH-n'n baoukh/zayr gehrn.

I love/ your eyes/ hands/ your tummy.

Was für schöne Locken!
Vahs fewr SHEHR-neh LOHK-'n!

What pretty curls.

So ein braves Mädchen!
Zoh ighn BRAH-vehs MEHD-sh'n!

What a good girl!   *

So ein braver Junge!
Zoh ighn BRAH-vuh YUHN-geh!

What a good boy!   *

Du bist grosszügig.
Doo bihst GROSS-tsewh-gihsh.

You are generous.

Ich habe dich gern.
Ihsh HAH-beh dihsh gehrn.

I like you.

Ich liebe dich.
Ihsh LEE-beh dihsh.

I love you.

Bravo.
BRAH-voh.

Bravo.

Gut gemacht!
Goot geh-MAKHT!

Well done.

Zugabe!
TSOO-gah-beh!

Encore!

Es gefällt mir, wie du so ruhig allein spielen
kannst.
Ess geh-FEHLT meer, vee doo zoh ROOH-ihsh
ahl-LIGHN SHPEE-l'n kahnst.

I like the way you play
quietly by yourself.

Versuch's noch einmal!
Fehr-ZOOKHS nokh IGHN-mahl!

Try again!

Gib nicht auf!
Ghip nihsht aouf!

Don't give up!

Was für eine prima Idee!
Vahs fewr IGH-neh PREE-mah EE-day!

What a great idea!

Du wirst immer besser !
Doo veerst IHM-muh BEHS-suh!

You're getting better
and better.

Ich war für deine Hilfe sehr dankbar!
Ihsh vahr fewr DIGH-neh HIHL-feh zayr
DANK-bahr!

I was very thankful for
your help.

Das ist lieb von dir.
Dahs ihst leep fonn deer.

That's sweet of you.

Du hast dein Zimmer geputzt.
Doo hahst dighn TSIHM-muh geh-PUHTS.

You cleaned your room.

Du bist mit den Händen sehr geschickt.
Doo bihst miht dain HEHN-d'n zayr
geh-SHIKHT.

You are good with your
hands.

Du kannst auf dich stolz sein!
Doo kahnst aouf dihsh shtohlz zighn!

You can be proud of
yourself.

67

Kleider machen Leute.   Clothes make the man.

EINKAUFEN   SHOPPING

This is the area of foreign language conversation which may be unpredictable.
When children are young, they enjoy speaking German. However, as they grow
more sensitive, they may not wish to appear "different" i.e., speaking a foreign
language that others might overhear. Assure them that you understand their
feelings. Resume speaking German outside the store or in the car. You might
suggest that you and they "play store" at home using German.

Willst du einkaufen gehen? Vihlst doo IGHN-kaou-f'n GAY-'n?	Do you want to go shopping?
Ich muss eine Liste machen. Ihsh muhs IGH-neh LIHS-teh MAH-kh'n.	I have to make a list.
Willst du mit mir.................... kommen: Vihlst doo miht meer............. KOHM-m'n:	Do you want to come with me:
zum Holzplatz (m), tsoom HOHLTS-plahts,	to the lumber yard,
zur Eisenwarenhandlung (f), tsoor IGH-z'n-vah-r'n-hahnt-luhng,	to the hardware store,

68

zur Gärtnerei,
tsoor GEHRT-neh-righ,

to the nursery,

zur Tankstelle,
tsoor TAHNK-shtel-leh,

to the gas station,

zum Spielwarengeschäft,
tsoom SHPEEL-vah-r'n-geh-sheft,

to the toy store,

zum (Herren) Frisör,
tsoom (HEHR-r'n) FREE-zehr,

to the barber,

zur Bäckerei,
tsoor BEKH-ehr-igh,

to the bakery,

zum Lebensmittelgeschäft,
tsoom LAY-behns-mit-t'l-geh-sheft,

to the grocery store,

zur Wäscherei,
tsoor VESH-eh-righ,

to the laundromat,

zum Sportgeschäft,
tsoom SHPORT-geh-sheft,

to the sports store,

zum Feinkostgeschäft,
tsoom FIGHN-kohst-geh-sheft,

to the delicatessen,

zum Kaufhaus,
tsoom KAOUF-haous,

to the department store,

zur Apotheke,
tsoor AH-poh-tay-keh,

to the drug store,

zum Fleischer,
tsoom FLIGH-shuh,

to the butcher shop,

zur Bank,
tsoor bahnk,

to the bank,

zum Bücherladen, tsoom BEWHK-uh-lah-d'n,	to the book store,
zum Schuhgeschäft, tsoom SHOO-geh-sheft,	to the shoe store,
zum Musikgeschäft, tsoom moo-ZEEK-geh-sheft,	to the music store,
zum Einkaufszentrum, tsoom IGHN-kaoufs-ts'n-truhm,	to the mall,
zur Post, tsoor pohst,	to the post office,
zum Videogeschäft. tsoom FIHD-eh-oh-geh-sheft.	to the video store.

Ich gehe zum Supermarkt.
Ihsh GAY-eh tsoom ZOO-puh-markht.

I am going to the supermarket.

Ich muss............ kaufen.
Ihsh muhs ....KAOU-f'n.

I have to buy...

Ich muss.................... zurückbringen.
Ihsh muhs....................tsoo-REWHK-brin-g'n.

I must return...
(bring something back)

Es gibt einen Ausverkauf.
Ess ghipt IGH-n'n AOUS-fehr-kaouf.

There's a sale.

Was kaufst du mit deinem Dollar?
Vahs kaoufst doo miht DIGH-n'm
DOHL-lahr?

What are you going to   *
buy with your dollar?

Nehmen wir /den Lift/ die Rolltreppe/.
NAY-m'n veer /dain lift / dee
ROHL-trehp-peh/.

Let's take /the elevator/
the escalator/.

70

Du kannst im Einkaufswagen/ sitzen/ bleiben/.
Doo kahnst im IGHN-kaoufs-vah-g'n/
ZIHT-ts'n/ BLIGH-b'n/.

You can / sit/ stay/ in the
shopping cart.   *

Steck deine Füsse durch die Öffnungen!
Shteck DIGH-neh FEWHS-seh
doorkh dee EHRF-nuhn-g'n!

Place your feet through
the openings.

Was darf es sein?
Vahs dahrf ess zighn?

Can I help you?

Ich hätte gern...
Ihsh HEHT-teh gehrn...

I'd like...

Wir können nicht zuviel Geld ausgeben.
Veer KEHRN-n'n nihsht TSOO-feel
gehlt AOUS-geh-b'n.

We cannot spend too
much money.

Wir können das nicht kaufen.
Veer KEHRN-n'n dahs nihsht KAOU-f'n.

We cannot buy that.

Mir ist das Geld etwas knapp.
Meer ihst dahs gehlt EHT-vahs k'napp.

I'm somewhat short of
money.

Ich habe kein Geld.
Ihsh HAH-beh kighn gehlt.

I do not have any money.

Das ist zu teuer.
Dahs ihst tsoo TOI-uh.

That's too expensive.

Vielleicht gibt es etwas billiger...
Feel-LIGHST ghipt ess EHT-vahs
BIHL-ih-guh...

Perhaps something
cheaper...

Das ist/ preiswert/ ein Sonderangebot/.
Dahs ihst/ PRIGHS-vehrt/ ighn ZOHN-
duh-ahn-geh-boht/.

That's a /good buy/ a
special offer/.

Ich brauche etwas Geld.
Ihsh BRAOU-sheh EHT-vahs gehlt.

I need some money.

71

Der Verkäufer/ Die Verkäuferin/ ist dort
drüben.
Dehr fehr-KOY-fuh/ Dee fehr-KOY-fuh-rihn/
ihst dohrt DREWH-b'n

The salesman/ saleswoman/
is over there.

Wieviel kostet es?
VEE-feel KOHS-teht ess?

How much is it?

Das macht 8 Mark 30.
Dahs makht akht mark DRIGH-sikh.

That will be 8 marks and
30 pfennigs.

Sollen wir es kaufen ?
ZOHL-l'n veer ess KAOU-f'n ?

Should we buy it?

Welche Grösse ist/ es/ dieser Mantel/?
VEHL-cheh GREHR-seh ihst/ ess/
DEE-zuh MAHN-tehl/?

What size is/ it/ this coat/?

Lass mich das sehen.
Lahs mihsh dahs ZAY-'n.

Let me see that.

Probiere es an.
Proh-BEER ess ahn.

Try it on.

Das ist /zu eng/ zu weit/.
Dahs ihst /tsoo ehnk/ tsoo vight/.

This is /too tight/ too
loose/.

Es ist (dir) /zu gross / zu klein/.
Ess ihst (deer) /tsoo grohss/ tsoo klighn/.

That is /too large/ too
small/ (for you).

Es steht dir gut.
Ess shteht deer goot.

It looks good on you.

Zähle dein Kleingeld.
TSEH-leh dighn KIGHN-gehlt.

Count your change.

Fass das nicht an.
Fahs dahs nihsht ahn.

Don't touch that.

Triff mich hier in einer Stunde!   Meet me here in an
Trihf mihsh heer in IGH-nuh SHTUHN-deh!   hour.

Bleib bei /der Mutti/ dem Vati/.   Stay with/ Mom/ Dad/.
Blighp bigh/ dehr MUHT-tee/ dehm FAH-tee/.

Meinst du, Vati hätte es gern?   Do you think Dad would
Mighnst doo, FAH-tee HETT-teh ess gehrn?   like it?

Hast du eine Einkaufstasche?   Do you have a shopping
Hahst doo IGH-neh IGHN-kaoufs-tash-eh?   bag?

Die Gänge sind voll.   The aisles are crowded.
Dee GEHN-geh zihnt fohl.

Wo ist/ die Kasse/ die Kassiererin/?   Where is/ the check-out/
Voh ihst/ dee KAHS-seh/ dee kahs-SIH-   the cashier/?
reh-rihn/?

Wir können einen Einkaufsbummel   We can go window
machen.   shopping.
Veer KEHRN-n'n IGH-n'n IGHN-kaoufs-
-buhm-mehl MAH-kh-'n.

/Der Ausgang/ der Eingang/ ist dort drüben.   /The exit/ the entrance/
/Dehr AOUS-gahng/ dehr IGHN-gahng/   is over there.
isht dohrt DREWH-b'n.

Wir suchen /Spielsachen/ Möbel/   We're looking for / toys/
Kleidung/ Sportausrüstung/.   furniture/ clothing/ sports
Veer ZOOK-h'n/ SHPEEL-zah-k'n/   equipment/.
MEHR-behl/ KLIGH-duhng/ SHPOHRT-
aous-rewhs-tung/.

Parkverbot!   No parking!
Parkh-fuh-BOHT!

wer nicht richtig faulenzen kann, kann auch nicht richtig arbeiten.

Work while you work, play while you play.

SPASS !   FUN !

If this chapter's pages don't have paint stains, water marks, tire tracks and gum sticking the pages together, you're not getting all there is to wring out of these pages! Be sure to write in some additional sentences and expressions you've learned elsewhere that are appropriate. I've found it helpful to put up sentences and phrases on 3 x 5 cards wherever I need them until the phrase is part of my thinking.

Du /darfst/ kannst/:	You/ are allowed to/ may/
Doo/dahrfst/ kahnst/:	can:

    im Garten spielen,
    im GAHR-t'n SHPEE-l'n,   play in the yard,

    zum Spielplatz gehen,
    tsoom SHPEEL-plats GAY-'n,   go to the playground,

    zum (Fussball, Baseball)-- feld gehen,
    tsoom (fuhss-bahl, BAYS-bahl)-- felht GAY-'n,   go to the (soccer, baseball) field,

    zu der Freundin gehen.
    tsoo dehr FROIN-dihn GAY-'n.   go to your friend's house.

Frag sie,
Frahk zee,

    Ask them,

ob sie spielen wollen,
ohp zee SHPEE-l'n VOHL-l'n,

    whether they want to play,

ob sie Arzt und Krankenschwester spielen wollen,
ohp zee artst oont KRAHN-k'n-shvehs-tuh
SHPEE-l'n VOLH-l'n,

    whether they want to play
    doctor and nurse,   *

ob sie Kaufladen spielen wollen,
ohp zee KAOUF-lah-d'n SHPEE-l'n VOHL-l'n,

    whether they want to play
    store,

ob sie am Computer spielen wollen,
ohp zee ahm kom-PEW-tuh SHPEE-l'n
VOHL-l'n,

    whether they want to play
    computer,

ob sie Verstecken spielen wollen.
ohp zee fehr-SHTEH-k'n SHPEE-l'n VOHL-l'n.

    whether they want to play
    hide and seek.

Darf ich mitspielen?
Dahrf ihsh MIHT-shpee-l'n?

    May I play with you?

       (FLUGZEUGE)   (AIRPLANES)   *

Pilot zum Kontrollturm.
Pih-LOHT tsoom kohn-TROHL-tuhrm.

    Pilot to control tower.

Bitte anschnallen.
BIT-teh AHN-shnahl-l'n.

    Please fasten your seatbelts.

Ich starte.
Ihsh SHTAHR-teh.

    I'm taking off.

Abdrosseln!
AHP-drohs-sehln!

    Throttle down!

Auf welcher Landebahn dürfen wir landen? | On which runway may we land?
Aouf VELH-cher LAHN-deh-bahn
DEWHR-f'n veer LAHN-d'n?

Der Treibstoff geht zur Neige! | We're running out of fuel!
Dehr TRIHP-shtoff gayt tsoor NIGH-geh!

Räumen Sie die Startbahn! | Clear the runway!
ROY-m'n zee dee SHTART-bahn!

Meine Maschine kann ein Looping machen. | My plane can do a loop.
MIGH-neh mah-SHEE-neh kahn ighn LOOP-ing MAK-kh'n.

Ich habe drei Wochen an meinem Modell gearbeitet. | I worked three weeks on my model.
Ihsh HAH-beh drigh VOKH-k'n ahn MIGH-n'm moh-DEHL geh-AHR-bigh-teht.

Wie lang ist der Flug nach Deutschland? | How long is the flight to Germany?
Vee lahng ihst dehr fluhk nakh DOITSCH-lahnt?

IM GARTEN / IN THE GARDEN

Geh /nach draussen/ ins Haus hinein/ und spiel! | Go/outside/ inside/ and play.
Geh/nakh DRAOU-z'n/ins haous hih-NIGHN / oont shpeel!

Spiel/ im Garten/ im Sandkasten/. | Play/ in the yard/ in the sand box/.
Shpeel / im GAHR-t'n/ im SAHNT-kahs-t'n/.

Willst du Seifenblasen blasen? | Do you want to blow soap bubbles?
Vihlst doo ZIGH-f'n-blah-s'n BLAH-s'n?

Spiel nicht im Dreck! | Don't play in the dirt.
Shpeel nihsht im drekh!

Plfücke die Blumen bitte nicht!
FLEWHK-keh dee BLOOM-e'n BIT-teh nihsht!

Please don't pick the
flowers!

Du kannst im Schwimmbad schwimmen,
wenn ich dabei bin.
Doo kahnst im SHVIMM-baht SHVIM-m'n,
vehn ihsh dah-BIGH bihn.

You can swim in the pool
if I am with you.

Spring vom Sprungbrett ab, wie ich
dir gezeigt habe.
Shpring fohm SHPRUNG-breht ahp, vee ihsh
deer geh-TSIHKT HAH-beh.

Jump off the diving board
as I have shown you.

Sei vorsichtig, wenn du in den Baum steigst.
Zigh FOHR-zish-tish, vehn doo in dain baoum
shtighkst.

Be careful when you are
climbing the tree.

Ihr beiden könnt im Karren sitzen.
EE-uh BIGH-d'n kehrnt im KAHR-r'n ZIHT-ts'n.

Both of you can sit in the
wagon.

Es gibt genug Platz für zwei.
Ess ghipt gay-NOOK plahts fewr tsvigh.

There's enough room for
two.

Kehre die Scherben auf!
KEH-reh dee SHERH-b'n aouf!

Sweep up the glass.

Kannst du das gebrochene Fenster ersetzen?
Kahnst doo dahs geh-BROCH-ehn-eh FEHNS-
tuh ehr-ZEHT-ts'n?

Can you replace the broken
window?

Verlasse den Garten nicht!
Fehr-LAHS-seh dain GAHR-t'n nihsht!

Don't leave the yard.

BASEBALL   *

(Note: The game of baseball does not exist in Germany. It is included here for its
American fans.)

Du bist dran!   It's your turn.(at bat)
Doo bihst drahn!   (You're at bat.)

/Fang/Wirf/ den Ball!   /Catch/ Throw/ the ball.
/Fahng/Veerf/ dain bahl!

Halte den Stock hinter dir!   Hold the bat behind you.
HAHL-teh dain shtokh HIN-tuh deer!

Behalte den Ball im Auge!   Keep your eye on the ball!
Beh-HAHL-teh dain bahl im AOU-geh!

Hau (mit dem Stock) los!   Swing (with the bat).
Haou (miht daim shtokh) lohs!

Du hast den Ball verpasst!   You missed the ball.
Doo hahst dain bahl fehr-PAHST!

Mach einen Punkt!   Score a run!
Makh IGH-n'n puhnkt !

Du hast den Ball sehr fest geschlagen!   You hit the ball very well.
Doo hahst dain bahl zayr fehst geh-SHLAH-g'n!

        (FAHRRADFAHREN)   BICYCLING   *

Stelle die Füsse auf die Pedale!   Put your feet on the
SHTEL-leh dee FEWHS-seh aouf dee   pedals.
peh-DAH-leh!

Tritt nicht so fest auf die Pedale!   Don't pedal so hard.
Triht nihsht zoh fehst aouf dee peh-DAH-leh!

Ich habe dich fest!   I've got a hold of you.
Ihsh HAH-beh dihsh fehst!

Versuch die Bilanz zu halten!   Try to keep your balance.
Fehr-ZOOKH dee bee-LAHNZ tsoo HAHL-t'n!

Lass mich mal versuchen!
Lahs mihsh mahl fehr-ZOOK-h'n!

Let me try!

Halte die Lenkstange fest!
HAHL-teh dee LEHNK-shtahn-geh fehst!

Hold on to the handlebars.

Immer geradeaus.
IHM-muh geh-RAH-deh-aous.

Go straight.

Bieg /nach rechts/ nach links/ ab!
Beek /nakh rekhts/ nakh leenks/ ahp!

Turn /to the right/ to the left/.

Tritt weiter!
Triht VIGH-tuh!

Keep pedaling.

Du fährst sehr schön rad!
Doo fehrst zayr shehrn raht!

You're riding your bicycle very well.

Fahr nicht in der Strasse rad!
Fahr nihsht in dehr SHTRAH-seh raht!

Don't ride your bicycle in the street.

Es gibt zuviel Verkehr.
Ess ghipt TSOO-feel fehr-KEHR.

There is too much traffic.

Du fährst zu schnell!
Doo fehrst tsoo shnell!

You're going too fast!

Bremse mal!
BREHM-seh mahl!

Put on the brakes!

Du musst einen Helm aufsetzen!
Doo muhst IGH-n'n hehlm AOUF-zeht-ts'n!

You need to put on your helmet!

(BRETTSPIELE)   BOARD GAMES   *

Willst du /Dame/ Schach/ ein Brettspiel/
spielen?
Vihlst doo /DAH-meh/ schakh/ ighn
BREHT-shpeel /SHPEE-l'n?

Do you want to play/ checkers/ chess/ a board game/?

79

Wer ist dran ?	Whose turn is it?
Vehr ihst drahn?	
Ich bin dran!	It's my turn.
Ihsh bihn drahn!	
Du bist dran!	It's your turn.
Doo bihst drahn!	
Ich würfle (jetzt)!	I'll throw the dice (now).
Ihsh VEWR-fleh (yehtst)!	
Ich will die blaue Figur (das blaue Stück).	I want the blue figure
Ihsh vihl dee BLAOU-eh FEE-guhr	(the blue piece). *
(dahs BLAOU-eh shtewkh).	
Dein Stück steht falsch.	Your piece is in the
Dighn shtewkh shteht fahlsh.	wrong place.
Du spielst nicht fair!	You aren't playing fairly.
Doo shpeelst nihsht fair!	
Du musst mich bezahlen.	You have to pay me.
Doo muhst mihsh beh-TSAH-l'n.	
Zieh /vorwärts/ rückwärts/.	Move /forwards/
Tsee /FOHR-vehrts/ REWHK-vehrts/.	backwards/.
Du hast /gewonnen/verloren/.	You have /won/ lost/.
Doo hahst /geh-VOHN-n'n/ fehr-LOH-r'n/.	

(BOOTE)	BOATS
Geh an Bord, bitte!	All aboard!
Gay ahn bohrt, BIT-teh!	
Wir verlassen den Hafen.	We're leaving the port.
Veer fehr-LAHS-s'n dain HAH-f'n.	

Wir fahren mit dem Schiff nach Deutschland.
Veer FAH-r'n miht daim shihf nakh
DOITSH-lahnt.

We're sailing to Germany.

Das Boot sinkt. Mann über Bord!
Dahs boht zinkt. Mahn EWH-buh bohrt!

The boat is sinking.
Man overboard!

Alle Mann von Bord!
AHL-leh mahn fonn bohrt!

Abandon ship!

Die Rettungsboote aussetzen!
Dee REHT-tungs-boh-teh AOUS-zeht-ts'n!

Lower the life boats!
*

Wir machen eine Bootfahrt.
Veer MAH-kh'n IGH-neh BOHT-fahrt.

We're going boating.

Langsamer fahren!
LAHNG-zah-muh FAH-r'n!

Slow down!

Ich fahre.
Ihsh FAH-reh.

I'll drive.

Du kannst wasserschilaufen.
Doo kahnst VAHS-suh-shee-laou-f'n.

You can water-ski.

Steig aus und schieb!
Shtighk aous oont sheep!

Get out and push!

Hol die Ruder!
Hohl dee ROOH-duh!

Get the oars!

Ich pulle!
Ihsh PUHL-leh!

I'll row.   *

(ZELTEN)   CAMPING   *

Wie lang wollen wir zelten?
Vee lahnk VOHL-l'n veer TSEHL-t'n?

How long do we want
to camp?

81

Wir brauchen ein neues Zelt. Veer BRAOU-hk'n ighn NOI-ehs tselt.	We need a new tent.
Dieses hat Löcher drin. DEE-zehs haht LERH-scher drihn.	This one has holes in it.
Es freut mich, dass wir unseren Wohnwagen noch haben. Ess froit mihsh, dahs veer OON-zur-'n VOHN-vah-g'n nokh HAH-b'n.	I am happy that we still have our camper.
Lass uns (zusammen) das Zelt aufschlagen. Lahs oons (tsoo-ZAHM-m'n) dahs tselt AOUF-shlah-g'n.	Let's pitch the tent (together).
Ich will einen Campingplatz direkt am See. Ihsh vihl IGH-n'n KAHM-ping-plahts dee-REKT ahm zay.	I want a campsite right on the lake.
Diejenigen, die einen Schlafsack haben, sollen im Freien schlafen. Dee-YAY-nee-g'n, dee IGH-n'n SHLAF-sakh HAH-b'n, ZOHL-l'n im FRIGH-'n SHLAH-f'n.	Those who have a sleep- ing bag should sleep out- doors.
Stell den Kocher auf! Shtell dain KAHK-huh aouf!	Set up the stove.

(AUTOS)	CARS *
Das Auto hat eine Panne gehabt. Dahs AOU-toh haht IGH-neh PAN-neh geh-HAPT.	The car broke down.
Es bewegt sich nicht mehr! Ess beh-VIGHT zihsh nihsht mayr!	It doesn't move any more.
Warum fährt das Auto nicht? Vah-ROOM fehrt dahs AOU-toh nihsht?	Why doesn't the car go?

Schieb das Auto!
Sheep dahs AOU-toh!

Auftanken!
AOUF-tahn-k'n!

Schau dem Öl, dem Wasser, der Batterie nach!
Shaou daim erhl, daim VAHS-suh, dehr
bah-tehr-REE nakh!

Fahr das Auto in die Garage!
Fahr dahs AOU-toh in dee gah-RAH-geh!

Gib Gas!
Ghip gas!

Mein Lieblingsauto ist................
Mighn LEEP-lings-aou-toh isht..............

Push the car!

Fill 'er up!

Check the oil, the
water, the battery!

Drive the car into the
garage!

Step on it!

My favorite car is........

(MALEN und ZUSAMMENSTELLEN)   COLOR and PASTE

Sie darf die Farbstifte gebrauchen!
Zee dahrf dee FAHRP-shtif-teh geh-BRAOU-hk'n!

She may use the crayons. *

Male die Sonne gelb!
MAH-leh dee ZOHN-neh gehlp!

Color the sun yellow.   *

Male den Vogel in der Farbe, die du willst.
MAH-leh dain FOH-gehl in dehr FAHR-beh,
dee doo vihlst.

Color the bird in the
color that you want.

Zeichne den Kreis, das Dreieck, das Rechteck
und das Quadrat so.
TSIGHKH-neh dain krighs, dahs DRIGH-ekh,
dahs RESHT-ekh oont dahs kwah-DRAHT zoh.

Draw the circle, the triangle,
rectangle and the square
like this.   *

Schneide dieses Bild aus der Zeitschrift!
SHNIGH-deh DEE-zehs bihlt aous dehr
TSIGHT-shrift!

Cut this picture out
of the magazine.

83

Klebe es vorsichtig aufs Papier!
KLEH-beh ess FOHR-zish-tish aoufs pah-PEER!

Paste it carefully onto the paper.

Falte das Papier!
FAHL-teh dahs pah-PEER!

Fold the paper!

Zerreiss das Papier nicht!
Tsehr-RIGHS dahs pah-PEER nihsht!

Don't tear the paper!

Rolle den Ton so aus!
ROHL-leh dain tohn zoh aous!

Roll out the clay like this!

Forme den Ton so!
FOHR-meh dain tohn zoh!

Form the clay like this.

Presse den Ton so (zusammen)!
PRES-seh dain tohn zoh (tsoo-ZAHM-m'n)!

Squeeze the clay (together) like this.

(COMPUTER)

COMPUTER

Willst du ein Computerspiel machen?
Vihlst doo ighn kom-PEW-tuh-speel MAH-kh'n?

Do you want to play a computer game?

Wir lassen das drucken!
Veer LAHS-s'n dahs DRUCK-k'n!

We'll have that printed.

Es gibt einen (Computer) Fehler!
Ess ghipt IGH-n'n (kom-PEW-tuh) FEH-luh!

There's a (computer) error.

Wir können mit dem Computer nach den Informationen suchen.
Veer KEHR-n'n miht daim kom-PEW-tuh nakh dain ihn-fohr-mah-TSIH-oh-n'n ZOOK-h'n.

We can search for information with the computer.

(PUPPEN)

DOLLS

Wie heisst die Puppe?
Vee highst dee PUHP-peh ?

What is your doll's name?

Füttere die Puppe! Zieh die Puppe an!
FEWT-teh-reh dee PUHP-peh! Tsee
dee PUHP-peh ahn!

Feed the doll. Dress the
doll.   *

Ich muss ihre Haare /bürsten/ kämmen/.
Ihsh muhs EE-reh HAH-reh /BEWHRS-t'n/
KEM-m'n/.

I have to /brush/ comb/
her hair.

Leg sie sanft hin!
Lehk zee zanft hin!

Put her down gently.

Schlepp sie nicht über den Boden!
Shlehp zee nihsht EWH-buh dain BOH-d'n!

Don't drag her on the floor.

Du kannst am Computer ein Kleid entwerfen.
Doo kahnst ahm kom-PEW-tuh ighn klight
ent-VEHR-f'n.

You can design a dress
on the computer.

(RATE MAL, WAS ES IST!)   GUESS WHAT !

Ich habe rote Kappen gern. Ich bin gross,
und ich stürme mit meinem Kopf an! Welches
Tier bin ich? (ein Stier)
Ihsh HAH-beh ROH-teh KAH-p'n gehrn. Ihsh
bihn grohss, oont ihsh SHTEWR-meh miht
MIGH-n'm kopf ahn! VEHL-ches teer bihn ihsh?
(ighn shteer).

I like red capes. I'm large, and
I charge with my head!
What animal am I? (a bull)

Ich sitze auf Seerosen. Ich sage: "quak-quak."
Ich kann meine Zunge weit und schnell aus-
strecken. Ich kann mit meiner Zunge allerlei
Insekten fangen. Welches Tier bin ich?
(ein Frosch)
Ihsh ZIHT-tseh aouf ZEE-roh-zen. Ihsh ZAH-geh
"kwak kwak." Ihsh kahn MIGH-neh TSUHN-geh
vight oont shnell AOUS-shtrehk-k'n. Ihsh kahn
miht MIGH-nuh TSUHN-geh AHL-luh-ligh
ihn-ZEHK-t'n FAHN-g'n. VEHL-ches teer
bihn ihsh? (ighn frohsh)

I sit on water-lilies. I say: "rip-it."
I can shoot out quickly and far
with my tongue. I can catch all
sorts of insects with my tongue.
Which animal am? (a frog)

85

Ich belle und knürre. Ich jage gern Katzen in
die Bäume. Welches Tier bin ich? (ein Hund)
Ihsh BELL-leh oont k'NEWR-reh. Ihsh YAH-
geh gehrn KAHT-ts'n in dee BOY-meh,
VEHL-ches teer bihn ihsh? (ighn huhnt)

I bark and growl. I like to
chase cats into trees.
Which animal am I ? (a dog)

Ich trage mein Baby in meinem Beutel. Ich habe
vier Beine, aber ich kann nicht laufen. Ich kann
aber weit springen. Welches Tier bin ich?
(ein Känguruh)
Ihsh TRAH-geh mighn BAY-beh in MIGH-n'm
BOI-tehl. Ihsh HAH-beh feer BIGH-neh,
AH-buh ihsh kahn nihsht LAOU-f'n. Ihsh kahn
AH-buh vight SHPRIN-g'n. VEHL-ches teer
bihn ihsh? (ighn KEHN-guh-ruh)

I carry my baby in my pouch.
I have four legs but I cannot
run. However, I can jump far.
Which animal am I?
(a kangaroo)

Ich stolziere und krähe. Ich habe Federn. Ich
wecke die Leute auf dem Bauernhof morgen
früh.
Welches Tier bin ich? (ein Hahn)
Ihsh SH'T'OHL-tseer-eh oont KREH-heh.
Ihsh HAH-beh FEH-dehrn. Ihsh VEHK-keh
dee LOI-teh aouf daim BAU-ern-hohf
MOHR-g'n frewh. (ighn hahn)

I strut and crow. I have
feathers. I waken the people
on the farm early in the
morning.
Which animal am I?
(a rooster)

(AUF DEM SPIELPLATZ)   ON THE PLAYGROUND

Geh und versteck dich!
Gay oont fehr-STEKH dihsh!

Go and hide!

Verschwinde!
Fehr-SCHVIN-deh!

Scram!

Wo bist du? Wo bin ich?
Voh bihst doo? Voh bihn ihsh?

Where are you?
Where am I?

Schaukle, aber schaukle nicht zu hoch!
SHAOU-kleh, AH-buh SHAOU-kleh
nihsht tsoo hokh!

Swing, but don't swing
too high!   *

Spring nicht von der Schaukel ab!
Shpring nihsht fonn dehr SHAOU-kehl ahp!

Don't jump off the swing!

Steh nicht auf der Schaukel!
Shteh nihsht aouf dehr SHAOU-kehl!

Don't stand on the swing!

Ich kann dich sanft schieben!
Ihsh kahn dihsh zanft SHEE-b'n!

I can push you gently!

Mach die Augen nicht zu!
Makh dee AOU-g'n nihsht tsoo!

Don't close your eyes!

Halte dich /an der Rutschbahn/am Karussell /fest!
HAHL-teh dihsh /ahn dehr RUTSH-bahn/ ahm kar-uh-SEHL /fehst!

Hold on to /the slide/ the merry-go-round /tightly!
                                                    *

Rutsch langsam hinunter!
Rutsh LAHNG-zahm hih-NUHN-tuh!

Slide down slowly!

Der Drache sinkt! Es gibt nicht genug Wind!
Dehr DRAH-keh zinkt! Ess ghipt nihsht gay-NOOK vihnt!

The kite is falling.
There's not enough wind.

Halte den Schwanz fest!
HAHL-teh dain shvahnts fehst!

Hold the tail tightly!

Willst du seilspringen?
Villst doo ZIGHL-shprin-g'n?

Do you want to jump rope?

Schiess die Murmeln in den Kreis.
Shees dee MUHR-m'ln in dain krighs.

Shoot the marbles into the the circle.

Blase den Luftballon auf!
BLAH-zeh dain LUFT-bah-lohn aouf!

Blow up the balloon.   *

Luft kommt aus dem Ballon!
Luft kohmt aous daim bah-LOHN!

Air is leaking from the balloon!

Hilfe! Feuer!
HIHL-feh! FOI-uh!

Help! Fire!

87

Alarmiere die Feuerwehr!
Ah-lah-MEER-eh dee FOI-uh-vehr!

Call the fire department!

Lass die Sirene heulen!
Lahs dee zee-REH-neh HOI-l'n!

Sound the siren!

Ich bin der Leiter. Ich mache, was ich will.
Ihsh bihn dehr LIGH-tehr. Ihsh MAH-kheh,
vahs ihsh vihl.

I'm the leader. I do what
I want.

Meine Schlittschuhe sind stumpf.
MIGH-neh SHLIT-shooh-eh zint shtumpf.

My skates are dull.   *

Man soll sie schärfen!
Mahn zohl zee SHEHR-f'n!

They need to be
sharpened.

Halte dich an mir fest! Ich helfe dir beim
schlittschuhlaufen.
HAHL-teh dihsh ahn meer fehst! Ihsh
HEHL-feh deer bighm SHLIT-shooh-laou-f'n.

Hold onto me. I'll help
you skate.

Schiebe mit dem linken Fuss!
SHEE-beh miht daim LIHN-k'n foos!

Push with the left foot!

Hebe den rechten Fuss!
HEH-beh dain RESH-t'n foos!

Lift the right foot!

Lauf mal eine Runde um die Eisbahn
schlittschuh!
Laouf mahl IGH-neh RUHN-deh uhm dee
IGHZ-bahn SHLIT-shooh!

Skate around the rink.

Du bist soweit, du kannst jetzt rückwärts
schlittschuhlaufen.
Doo bihst zoh-VIGHT, doo kahnst yehtst
REWHK-vehrts SHLIT-shooh-laou-f'n.

You're ready to skate
backwards.

Lauf mit dem Ball!
Laouf miht daim bahl!

Run with the ball!

Fass den Ball mit den Händen nicht an!
Fahs dain bahl miht dain HENN-d'n nihsht ahn!

Don't touch the ball
with your hands!

Schiess den Ball ins Tor!
Shees dain bahl ins tohr.

Shoot the ball into the
goal!   *

Lauf dich frei! Bleib in Bewegung!
Laouf dihsh frigh! Blighp in beh-VEH-gung!

Get free! Move around!

Du hast ein Tor geschossen!
Doo hahst ighn tohr geh-SHOHS-s'n!

You have scored a goal!

Du hast daneben geschossen! Kein Tor!
Doo hahst dah-NEH-b'n geh-SHOHS-s'n!
Kighn tohr!

You shot wide! No goal!

Spiel (mir) den Ball zu!
Shpeel (meer) dain bahl tsoo!

Pass the ball (to me)!

Das hat nicht geklappt!
Dahs haht nihsht geh-KLAPPT!

That didn't work!

Aus! Drin! Abseits!
Aous! Drihn! AHP-zights!

Out! In! Off sides!

(RUHIGE SPIELE)

QUIET GAMES

Mach ein ruhiges Spiel und entspanne dich!
Makh ighn ROOH-ih-gehs shpeel oont
ent-SHPAN-neh dihsh!

Play a quiet game and rest!

Legen wir dieses Puzzleteil dahin!
LEH-g'n veer DEE-zehs PAZ-zel-tighl dah-HIN!

Let's put this puzzle piece
in there.   *

Meinst du, dieses Teil kommt hier 'rein?
Mighnst doo, DEE-zehs tighl kohmt heer righn?

Do you think this piece
goes here?

Dieses Teil passt nicht 'rein.
DEE-zehs tighl pahst nihsht righn.

This piece doesn't fit.

89

Welches Teil fehlt?
VEHL-ches tighl faylt?

Which piece is missing?

Dieses Puzzle ist /zu leicht/zu schwer/!
DEE-zehs PAZ-zel ihst /tsoo lighkt /tsoo shvehr/!

This puzzle is too /easy/ hard/.

Schau zum Fenster hinaus!
Shaou tsoom FEHNS-tuh hee-NAOUS!

Look out the window!

Was siehst du?
Vahs zeehst doo?

What do you see?

Willst du (mit mir) Karten spielen?
Vihlst doo (miht meer) KAHR-t'n SHPEE-l'n?

Do you want to play cards (with me)?

Du kannst deine Briefmarkensammlung
durchsortieren!
Doo kahnst DIGH-neh BREEF-mahr-k'n-zahm-
-lung DOORKH-zohr-teer-e'n!

You can sort your stamp collection.

(ZÜGE und LASTWAGEN)

TRAINS and TRUCKS

Alles einsteigen, bitte!
AHL-lehs IGHN-shtigh-g'n, BIT-teh!

All aboard!

Die Fahrkarten, bitte!
Dee FAHR-kahr-t'n, BIT-teh!

Tickets, please!

Was kostet die Fahrt?
Vahs KOHS-teht dee fahrt?

What does the trip cost?

Ich fahre /rückwärts/ vorwärts.
Ihsh FAH-reh /REWHK-vehrts/FOHR-vehrts/.

I'm driving /backwards/ forwards/.

Lieferst du Öl mit deinem Ölwagen?
LEE-fehrst doo erl miht DIGH-n'm ERL-vah-g'n?

Are you delivering oil with your oil truck?

Dieser ist kein Ölwagen, sondern ein Viehwagen.
DEE-zuh ihst kighn ERL-vah-g'n, zohn-DERN
ighn FEE-vah-g'n.

This is not an oil truck; rather a cattle truck.

90

Ich lade meinen Lastwagen mit Sand.
Ihsh LAH-deh MIGH-n'n LAHST-vah-g'n
miht zahnt.

I'm loading my truck
with sand.   *

Ich habe den offenen Lieferwagen
(mit Vierradantrieb) sehr gern.
Ihsh HAH-beh dain OHF-f'n LEE-fuh-vah-g'n
(miht FEER-raht-ahn-treep) zayr gehrn.

I like the (4 x 4) pick-up.

Wenn ich den Führerschein habe, will ich...
Vehn ihsh dain FEWHR-uh-shighn HAH-beh,
vihl ihsh...

When I have my license,
I want...

Viel Spass!
Feel shpahs!

Have fun!

Viel Vergnügen!
Feel fehrk-NEWH-g'n!

Enjoy yourself!

Je mehr Leute, je mehr Glück. The more, the merrier.

SAMSTAGNACHMITTAG   SATURDAY AFTERNOON

The opportunities for using German on Saturdays are unlimited. Saturdays were made for German! Chores to be done using German, visits to friends using German, shopping, outings, sports. The list is endless as you can see.

Gehen wir /ins Kino/ zum Einkaufszentrum/.
GAY-'n veer /ins KEE-noh/ tsoom
IGHN-kaoufs-ts'n-truhm/.

Let's go /to the movies/
to the mall/.

Dürfen_____und _____mitkommen?
DEWHR-f'n_____ oont_____
MIHT-kohm-m'n?

May _____ and_____
come along?

Ich möchte lieber zum Spielplatz gehen.
Ihsh MEHRSH-teh LEE-buh tsoom SHPEEL-
plahts GAY-'n.

I'd rather go to the playground.

Es macht mehr Spass.
Ess makht mayr shpahs.

It is more fun.

Bist du mit deinen Hausarbeiten fertig?
Bihst doo miht DIGH-n'n HAOUS-
ahr-bigh-t'n FEHR-tikh?

Are you finished with your
chores?

Es gibt eine Zugausstellung.
Ess ghipt IGH-neh TSOOG-aous-shtel-lung.

There is a train exhibit.   *

Es gibt Schülertheater.
Ess ghipt SHEWH-luh-tay-ah-tuh.

There is a school play.

Es gibt Marionettentheater in der Bibliothek.
Ess ghipt mah-ree-oh-NET-t'n-tay-ah-tuh
in dehr bib-lee-oh-TEHK.

There's a puppet show at
the library.

Es gibt eine Gartenausstellung.
Ess ghipt IGH-neh GAHR-t'n-aous-shtel-lung.

There is a garden show.

Es gibt eine Autoausstellung in der Sporthalle.
Ess ghipt IGH-neh AOU-toh-aous-shtel-lung in
dehr SHPORT-hahl-luh.

There's a car show at the
coliseum.

Wir nehmen /die U-Bahn/ den Bus/.
Veer NAY-m'n /dee OO-bahn/dain bus/.

We'll take / the subway/
the bus/.

Können wir im Restaurant essen?
KEHRN-'n veer im rehst-aou-RAHNT
ESS-'n?

Can we eat out?

Ich will /im Restaurant/ im Schnellimbiss/ essen.
Ihsh vihl /im rehst-aou-RAHNT/ im
SHNELL-ihm-biss /ESS-'n.

I want to eat in a/ restaurant/
fast food place/.

Du hast einen Termin beim Zahnarzt.
Doo hahst IGH-n'n tehr-MEEN bighm
TSAHN-artst.

You have an appointment at
the dentist's.

Deine Zahnspangen müssen eingestellt werden.
DIGH-neh TSAHN-shpahn-g'n MEWHS-s'n
IGN-geh-shtellt VEHR-d'n.

Your braces need to be
adjusted.

Nein,du darfst deine Haare nicht /blond/ rot/ färben!
Nighn, doo dahrfst DIGH-neh HAH-reh nihsht/
/blohnt/ roht /FEHR-b'n!

No, you aren't allowed to dye
your hair/ blond/ red/!

93

Steig ins Auto ein! Wir machen eine kleine Fahrt.
Shtighk ins AOU-toh ighn! Veer MAH-kh'n
IGH-neh KLIGH-neh fahrt.

Get in the car! We'll go for
a short ride.

Ruf an, und wir gehen /rollbrettfahren/
rollschuhfahren/.
Roof ahn, oont veer GAY-'n /ROHL-brett-
fah-r'n/ ROHL-shooh-fah-r'n/.

Call up and we'll go /skate-
boarding/ roller skating/.   *

Drachenfliegen würde Spass machen.
DRAH-kh'n-flee-g'n VEWHR-deh shpahs
MAH-kh'n.

Hang gliding would be
fun.

Hören wir mal meine neue CD an!
HEHR-'n veer mahl MIGH-neh NOI-eh
TSEE-dee ahn!

Let's listen to my new CD!

Ich möchte lieber angeln gehen.
Ihsh MEHRSH-teh LEE-buh AHN-gehln GAY-'n.

I would rather go fishing.

Wir haben den Köder, die Angelhaken und
das Netz.
Veer HAH-b'n dain KEHR-duh, dee AHN-gel-
hah-k'n oont dahs nets.

We've got the bait, the
hooks and the net.

Du hast die Angelrute vergessen!
Doo hahst dee AHN-gel-ruh-teh fehr-GEHS-'n!

You forgot the fishing rod.
                                    *

Möchtest du angeln gehen?
MEHRSH-t'st doo AHN-geln GAY-'n?

Would you like to go
fishing?

Ich habe einen Fisch gefangen!
Ihsh HAH-beh IGH-n'n fish geh-FAHN-g'n!

I caught a fish!

Können wir das Baumhaus nicht fertigmachen?
KEHRN-n'n veer dahs BAOUM-haous nihsht
FEHR-tikh-mah-kh'n?

Can't we finish the tree
house?

Ich hole den Hammer, Nägel,die Säge und Bretter.
Ihsh HOH-leh dain HAHM-muh, NEH-gehl,
ZEH-geh oont BREHT-tuh.

I'll get the hammer, nails,
the saw and boards.

94

Triff mich im Garten hinter dem Haus.
Trihf mihsh im GAHR-t'n HIN-tuh daim haous.

Meet me in the back yard.

Gehen wir auf den Dachboden!
GAY-'n veer aouf dain DASH-boh-d'n!

Let's go to the attic.

Schauen wir das Fussballspiel (im Fernsehen) an!
SHAOU-'n veer dahs FOOS-bahl-shpeel (im
FEHRN-zay-'n) ahn!

Let's watch the soccer match
(on TV).

Lesen wir Comic-hefte!
LAY-z'n veer KOH-mick-hehf-teh!

Let's read comic-books.

Gehen wir /zum Strand/ zum See/!
GAY-'n veer /tsoom shtrahnt/ tsoom zay/!

Let's go /to the beach/ to the
lake/.

Gehen wir /zum Ozean/zum Schwimmbad/!
GAY-'n veer /tsoom OH-tsee-ahn/ tsoom
SHVIMM-baht/!

Let's go /to the ocean/ to the
pool/.   *

Gehen wir schwimmen!
GAY-'n veer SHVIM-m'n!

Let's go swimming.

Gehen wir wasserschilaufen!
GAY-'n veer VAHS-suh-shee-laou-f'n!

Let's go water-skiing.

Ich bringe die Badetücher,
Ihsh BRIN-geh dee BAH-teh-tewh-huh,

I'll bring the towels,

   den Sonnenschirm,
   dain ZOHN-n'n-shirm,

   the umbrella,

   den Liegestuhl, den Eimer und die Schaufel.
   dain LEE-geh-shtool, dain IGH-muh
   oont dee SHAOU-fehl.

   the beach chair, the pail
   and the shovel.   *

/Das Wasser/ der Himmel/ ist klar.
/Dahs VAHS-suh/ dehr HIHM-mehl /ihst klahr.

The /water/ sky/ is clear.

95

Breite die Decke /in der Sonne/ im Schatten/ aus!
BRIGH-teh dee DEK-keh /in dehr ZOHN-neh/
im SHAH-t'n /aous!

Spread the blanket /in the
sun /in the shade/.

Das Wasser ist /stürmisch/ ruhig/ warm/ kalt/.
Dahs VAHS-suh ihst /SHTEWRM-ihsh/
ROOH-ihsh/ vahrm/ kahlt/.

The water is / rough/ calm/
warm/ cold/.

Wir können die Luftmatratze teilen.
Veer KERHN-n'n dee LUFT-mah-trah-tseh
TIGH-l'n.

We can share the air-mattress.

Du darfst nicht ins Wasser zurück!
Doo dahrfst nihsht ins VAHS-suh
tsoo-REWHK!

You aren't allowed back in
the water.

Du hast gerade gegessen!
Doo hahst geh-RAH-deh geh-GEHS-'n!

You have just eaten!

Es ist dir zu kalt.
Ess ihst deer tsoo kahlt.

You're too cold.

Es gibt hier Quallen!
Ess ghipt heer KVAHL-l'n!

There are jelly fish here!

Es wird schon spät!
Ess veert shown shpeht!

It's getting late.

Warum suchst du nicht Muscheln?
Vah-ROOM zuchst doo nihsht MUSH-eln?

Why don't you look for
shells?   *

Warum baust du nicht eine Sandburg?
Vah-ROOM baoust doo nihsht IGH-neh
ZAHNT-burk?

Why don't you build a
sand castle?   *

Warum legst du dich nicht auf die Decke hin?
Vah-ROOM lehkst doo dihsh nihsht aouf dee
DEH-keh hihn?

Why don't you lie down
on the blanket?

96

Warum schaust du dir die Vögel nicht an?
Vah-ROOM shaoust doo deer dee FEHR-gehl
nihsht ahn?

Why don't you watch the
birds?

Pass auf deine Schwester auf!
Pahs aouf DIGH-neh SHVEHS-tuh aouf!

Keep an eye on your sister!

Wo ist das Sonnenöl?
Voh ihst dahs ZOHN-nen-erl?

Where is the suntan lotion?

Wo ist die Sonnenbrille?
Voh ihst dee ZOHN-nen-brihl-leh?

Where are the sun-glasses?　*

Wo sind das Essen und die Getränke?
Voh zint dahs ESS-'n oont dee geh-TREHN-keh?

Where are the lunch and the
drinks?

Was für ein schöner Tag zum Schwimmengehen!
Vahs fewr ighn SHEHR-nuh tahk tsoom
SHVIM-men-gay-'n!

What a beautiful day for
swimming!

Was für ein schöner Tag zum Schilaufen!
Vahs fewr ighn SHEHR-nuh tahk tsoom
SHEE-laou-f'n!

What a beautiful day for
skiing!　　　　*

Wir brauchen nicht, ...zu mieten!
Veer BRAOU-hk'n nihsht,...........tsoo MEE-t'n!

We don't need to rent:

　die Schier, (dee SHEE-uh),
　die Schistöcke, (dee SHEE-shtehr-keh),
　die Schistiefel. (dee SHEE-shtee-fehl).

　the skis,
　the ski poles,
　the ski boots.

Wir haben unsere eigene Ausrüstung.
Veer HAH-b'n OON-zeh-reh IGH-geh-neh
AOUS-rewhs-tung.

We have our own equipment.

Meine Ausrüstung muss eingestellt werden.
MIGH-neh AOUS-rewhs-tung muhs
IGHN-geh-shtellt VEER-d'n.

My equipment needs to be
adjusted.

97

Der Schnee ist /zu weich/ zu hart/.
Dehr shnay ihst /tsoo vighsh/ tsoo hahrt/.

The snow is /too soft/ too hard/.

Wieviel kostet eine Sesselliftkarte?
VEE-feel KOHS-teht IGH-neh ZEHS-sehl-lift-kahr-teh?

How much is a chairlift ticket?

Wo ist der Schalter?
Voh ihst dehr SHAHL-tuh?

Where is the ticket office?

Geh nicht bis an die Spitze!
Gay nihsht bihs ahn dee SHPIT-tseh!

Don't go to the top!

Der Hang ist (dir) zu steil!
Dehr hahng ihst (deer) tsoo shtighl!

The hill is too steep (for you)!

Das ist gefährlich! Nicht zu schnell!
Dahs ihst geh-FEHR-lish! Nihsht tsoo shnell!

That's dangerous! Not too fast!

Was für Form!
Vahs fewr form!

What form!

Bist du hungrig? Ist es dir kalt?
Bihst doo HUHN-grish? Ihst ess deer kahlt?

Are you hungry? Are you cold?

Ich bin hungrig. Es ist mir kalt.
Ihsh bihn HUHN-grish. Ess ihst meer kahlt.

I am hungry. I am cold.

Bist du müde?
Bihst doo MEWH-deh?

Are you tired?

Gehen wir nach drinnen,
GAY-'n veer nakh DRIHN-n'n,

Let's go inside,

um uns auszuruhen,
uhm oons AOUS-tsoo-rooh-'n,

in order to rest,

um zu essen,
uhm tsoo ESS-'n,

in order to eat,

98

um uns aufzuwärmen.
uhm oons AOUF-tsoo-vehr-m'n.

in order to warm up.

Hier ist es angenehm warm.
Heer ihst ess AHN-geh-naym varhm.

It's pleasant and warm here.

Machen wir einige Fotos!
MAH-kh'n veer IGH-neh-geh FOH-tos!

Let's take some photos!

Wann fahren wir weg?
Vahn FAH-r'n veer vek?

When are we leaving?

Es ist Zeit, nach Hause zu gehen.
Ess ihst tsight, nakh HAOU-zeh tsoo GAY-'n.

It is time to go home.

Es gibt (sicher) viel Verkehr.
Ess ghipt (ZISH-huh) feel fehr-KEHR.

There will (certainly) be
a lot of traffic.

Sei sicher, dass du alles hast.
Zigh ZISH-huh, dahs doo AHL-lehs hahst.

Be sure that you have
everything.

Hast du Spass gehabt?
Hahst doo shpahs geh-HAHPT?

Did you have a good time?

Ich habe Spass gehabt.
Ihsh HAH-beh shpahs geh-HAHPT.

I had a good time.

Je mehr Kinder, desto mehr Glück. It takes children to make a happy home.

AUFRUFE	EXCLAMATIONS
O.K. Alles klar! Ist gut. Oh kay. AHL-lehs klahr! Ihst goot!	Okay. No problem ! Fine by me.
Wie dumm! Vee duhmm!	How silly!
Ich bin /traurig/ glücklich/. Ihsh bihn /TRAOU-rish/GLEWHK-lish/.	I am /sad/ happy/.
Es freut uns, du hast gewonnen. Ess froit oons, doo hahst geh-VOHN-n'n.	We are glad that you won.
Hilfe! HIHL-feh!	Help!
Vorsicht! FOHR-zisht!	Careful!
Es tut mir leid! Ich bin Schuld daran. Ess toot meer light! Ihsh bihn shuhlt dah-RAHN.	I'm sorry. It's my fault.
Quatsch! Kvatsh!	Rubbish! Nonsense!

100

Warum dauert es so lang?
Vah-ROOM DAOU-ert ess zoh lahng?

Why is it taking so long?

Schau, schau!
Shaou, shaou!

Well, what do you know!

Ist das (wirklich) so?
Ihst dahs (VIHRK-lish) zoh?

Is that (really) so?

Das ist egal!
Dahs ihst eh-GAHL!

Who cares?

Das ist mir völlig gleich!
Dahs ihst meer VERHL-ish glighsh!

I don't care.

Es ist mir egal.
Ess ihst meer eh-GAHL.

It's all the same to me.

Das geht dich nicht an.
Dahs gayt dihsh nihsht ahn.

That doesn't concern you.

Wer weiss?
Vehr vighs?

Who knows?

Das ist (nicht) wichtig.
Dahs ihst (nihsht) VISH-tish.

That's (not) important.

Sicher (nicht)!
ZISH-huh (nihsht) !

Of course (not)!
Certainly (not)!

Sicher! Richtig!
ZISH-huh! RIHSH-tikh!

Sure! Correct!

Schluss damit!
Shluhs dah-MIHT!

Matter closed!

Das meine ich auch!
Dahs MIGH-neh ihsh aoukh!

I agree.

101

Wie interessant!
Vee ihn-tehr-ehs-SAHNT!

How interesting!

Wie lustig! Das ist nicht lustig!
Vee LUHS-tish! Dahs ihst nihsht LUHS-tish!

How funny! That is not funny!

Unsinn!
UHN-zihnn!

Nonsense!

Welch ein Glück!
Velsh ighn glewhk!

What luck!   *

Du hast aber Glück!
Doo hahst AH-buh glewhk!

Lucky you!

Wie schrecklich!
Vee SHREHK-lish!

How awful!

Das ist schade. Es ist eine Schande!
Dahs ihst SHAH-deh. Ess ihst IGH-neh
SHAN-deh!

It's a shame. What a pity.

Das ist unglaublich!
Dahs ihst uhn-GLAOUP-lish!

That is unbelievable
(extraordinary)!

Wie nett! Wie schön!
Vee net! Vee sherhn!

How kind! How nice!

Wunderbar! Prima!
VUHN-duh-bahr! PREE-mah!

Wonderful! Marvelous!
Great! Terrific!

Das ist kein Witz!
Dahs ihst kighn vihts!

That's no joke!

Ich hoffe (nicht)!
Ihsh HOHF-feh (nihsht)!

I hope (not)!

Ich meine ja! Ich meine nein!
Ihsh MIGH-neh yah! Ihsh MIGH-neh nighn!

I think so! I think not!

102

Ach so!
Ahk zoh!

Oh, I see!

Ist das (dir) ganz klar?
Ihst dahs (deer) gants klahr?

Is that completely clear
(to you)?

(Hab) keine Sorge! (Hab) keine Angst!
(Hahp) KIGH-neh ZOHR-geh! (Hahp)
KIGH-neh ankst!

Don't worry! Don't be
afraid!

Beruhige dich!
Beh-ROOH-ih-geh dihsh!

Calm down!

Bitte sehr.
BIT-teh sayr.

Here it is. There you are.

Du bist zwischen zwei Feuern!
Doo bihst TSVIHSH-e'n tsvigh FOI-ern!

You're between the devil
and the deep blue sea.

Es wird schon gut gehen!
Ess veert shown goot GAY-'n!

It will be all right.

Das stimmt (nicht).
Dahs shtihmmt (nihsht).

It's (not) right.

Das ist nicht nötig.
Dahs ihst nihsht NEHR-tish.

That's not necessary.

Das sollst du lieber nicht!
Dahs zohlst doo LEE-buh nihsht!

You'd better not!

So ein Durcheinander!
Zoh ighn DOORKH-ighn-ahn-duh!

What a mess!

Genug davon!
Gay-NOOK dah-FOHN!

Enough of that!

Ich habe die Nase voll!
Ihsh HAH-beh dee NAH-seh fohl!

I'm fed up! I've had
it up to here!

103

Was können wir machen?
Vahs KEHRN-'n veer MAH-kh'n?

What's to be done?
(What can we do)?

Das ist wahr, oder?
Dahs ihst vahr, OH-duh?

That's true, don't you think?

Weisst du, ------
Vighst doo, -----

You know, ---

Jawohl!
Yah-VOHL!

Yes, indeed!

Sag bloss! Echt?
Zahk blohss! Esht?

You don't say! Really?

Wie sonst!
Vee zohnst!

As usual.

Was für ein Niesen! Zum Wohl!
Vahs fewr ighn NEE-s'n. Tsoom vohl!

What a sneeze!
God bless you!

Was ist (mit dir) los?
Vahs ihst (miht deer) lohs?

What's wrong (with you)?

Es ist nichts los.
Ess ihst nihshts lohs.

Nothing is the matter.

Warum meckerst du?
Vah-ROOM MECK-kehrst doo?

Why are you complaining?

Warum weinst du?
Vah-ROOM vighnst doo?

Why are you crying?

Schau!
Shaou!

Look!

Gefahr! Vorsicht! Bissiger Hund!
Guh-FAHR! FOHR-zihsht! BIHS-sih-guh huhnt!

Danger! Caution!
Biting dog!

Um Himmels Willen!   For goodness sake!
Uhm HIHM-mels VIHL-l'n!

Wie kann ich so dumm sein!   How stupid of me!
Vee kahn ihsh zoh duhm zighn!

Das ist nichts zum Lachen!   That is no laughing matter!
Dahs ihst nihshts tsoom LAH-ch'n!

Das geschieht dir recht!   It serves you right!
Dahs geh-SHEEHT deer rekht!

Du musst das nicht sagen!   You must not say that!
Doo muhst dahs nihsht ZAH-g'n!

Gott behüte!   God forbid!
Goht beh-HEWH-teh!

Warum in aller Welt!   Why on earth!
Vah-ROOM in AHL-luh vehlt!

Es ist unermesslich!   It's immense!
Ess ihst uhn-uh-MESS-lish!

In Ordung!   That's fine.
In OHRD-nuhng!

Ich auch!   Me too!
Ihsh aoukh!

Wie meinst du das?   What do you mean?
Vee mighnst doo dahs?

Was willst du damit sagen?   What are you trying to say?
Vahs vihlst doo dah-MIHT ZAH-g'n?

Leben und leben lassen. Live and let live.

GEBURTSTAGSFEIER

Alles Gute zum Geburtstag!
AHL-lehs GOO-teh tsoom geh-
BUHRTS-tahk!

Was wünschst du dir zum Geburtstag?
Vahs vewnschst doo deer tsoom
geh-BUHRTS-tahk?

Möchtest du eine Geburtstagsparty haben?
MEHRSH-t'st doo IGH-neh geh-BUHRTS-
tahks-par-tee HAH-b'n?

Wir laden deine Freunde ein!
Veer LAH-d'n DIGH-neh FROIN-deh ighn!

Wen willst du einladen?
Vehn vihlst doo IGHN-lah-d'n?

Vielleicht können wir ein Picknick haben!
Feel-LIGHST KEHRN-'n veer ighn
PICK-nick HAH-b'n!

BIRTHDAY PARTY

Happy Birthday!

What would you like for
your birthday?

Would you like to have a
birthday party?

We'll invite your friends.

Whom do you want to
invite?

Maybe we could have a
picnic!

Bei der Party gibt es:
Bigh dehr PAR-tee ghipt ess:

    Eis, Spiele, Luftballons,
    Ighz, SHPEE-leh, LUFT-bahl-lohns,

    Hüte, Geschenke, einen Geburtstagskuchen.
    HEWH-teh, geh-SHEHN-keh, IGH-n'n
    geh-BUHRTS-tahks-kooh-h'n.

Wo willst du die Party haben?
Voh vihlst doo dee PAR-tee HAH-b'n?

    zu Hause, im Park,
    tsoo HAOU-zeh, im park,

    im Restaurant oder am Strand?
    im rehs-taou-RAHNT OH-duh ahm shtranht?

Ich will eine Party mit allen meinen Freunden.
Ihsh vihl IGH-neh PAHR-tee miht AHL-l'n
MIGH-n'n FROIN-d'n.

Ich habe dir eine Geburtstagskarte und
ein Geschenk gekauft.
Ihsh HAH-beh deer IGH-neh geh-BUHRTS-
tahks-kahr-teh oont ighn geh-SHEHNK
geh-KAOUFT.

Wie alt bist du? Ich weiss es nicht.
Vee ahlt bihst doo? Ihsh vighs ess nihsht.

Ich bin fünf Jahre alt.
Ihsh bihn fewhnf YAH-reh ahlt.

Mein Geburtstag ist am zehnten (10.) Mai.
Mighn geh-BUHRTS-tahk ihst ahm ZEHN-
tehn migh.

At the party we'll have:

    ice cream, games,
    balloons,

    hats, presents, a birthday
    cake.   *

Where do you want to have
the party?

    at home, in the park,

    in a restaurant or at the
    beach?

I want a party with all
my friends.

I bought you a birthday
card and a present.

How old are you? I don't
know.

I am five years old.

My birthday is on May 10.

Wann hast du Geburtstag?
Vahn hahst doo geh-BUHRTS-tahk?

When is your birthday?

Wie viele Kerzen?
Vee FEE-leh KEHR-ts'n?

How many candles?

Wir wollen sie zählen!
Veer VOHL-l'n zee TSEH-l'n!

Let's count them!

Blase die Kerzen aus!
BLAH-zeh dee KEHR-ts'n aous!

Blow out the candles!

Schneide den Kuchen an!
SHNIGH-deh dain KOOH-h'n ahn!

Cut the cake!

Ich will Schokoladeneis, Erdbeereis, Vanilleeis.
Ihsh vihl shoh-koh-LAH-d'n-ighs, EHRT-behr-ighs, feh-NIHL-eh-ighs.

I want chocolate ice   *
cream, strawberry ice
cream, vanilla ice cream.

Teile den Kuchen in acht Stücke!
TIGH-leh dain KOOH-h'n in ahkt SHTEWH-keh!

Divide the cake into eight
pieces.

Was für eine super Party!
Vahs fewr IGH-neh ZOO-puh PAR-tee!

What a great party!

Darf ich jetzt meinen Führerschein bekommen?
Dahrf ihsh yehtst MIGH-n'n FEWHR-ehr-shighn beh-KOHM-men?

Now can I get my driver's
license?

Morgen ist auch noch ein Tag.   Tomorrow is another day.

ZUBETTGEHEN   BEDTIME

This is a fine time to read a story or book in German to your child. The language he hears before going to sleep will linger in his mind during the night. This might also be a golden opportunity to learn and recite prayers in German.

Was für ein Gähnen!   What a yawn!
Vahs fewr ighn GEH-n'n!

Du gähnst!   You're yawning.
Doo gehnst!

Bist du /müde/ schläfrig/?   Are you /tired/ sleepy?
Bihst doo /MEWH-deh/ SHLEHF-rish/?

Ich bringe dich zu Bett.   I'm bringing you to bed.
Ihsh BRIHN-geh dihsh tsoo bett.

Willst du, dass ich dich zu Bett bringe?   Do you want me to bring you
Vihlst doo, dahs ihsh dihsh tsoo bett   to bed?
BRIHN-geh?

Geh, hol dein Buch!   Go, get your book!
Gay, hohl dighn boohk!

109

Ich lese dir eine Geschichte vor,
Ihsh LAY-zeh deer IGH-neh geh-SCHISH-teh fohr,

I'll read you a story,

...bevor du zu Bett gehst.
...buh-FOHR doo tsoo bett gayst.

...before you go to bed.

Siehst du dir das Fernsehen an?
Zeehst doo deer dahs FEHRN-zay-'n ahn?

Are you watching TV?

Zieh doch deine Kleidung aus!
Tsee dokh DIGH-neh KLIGH-dung aous!

Take off your clothes.

Zieh dir den Schlafanzug an!
Tsee deer dain SCHLAHF-ahn-tsoog ahn!

Put on your pajamas.   *

Häng dein Hemd auf!
Hehnk dighn hemt aouf!

Hang up your shirt.

Räume deine Kleidung auf!
ROY-meh DIGH-neh KLIGH-dung aouf!

Clean up your clothes!

Diese Socken müssen gewaschen werden.
DEE-zeh ZOCK-k'n MEWHS-s'n geh-VAH-sh'n VEHR-d'n.

These socks need to be washed.   *

Bist du soweit, zu Bett zu gehen?
Bihst doo zoh-VIGHT, tsoo bett tsoo GAY-'n?

Are you ready for bed?

Sag dem Vati „Gute Nacht!"
Zahk daim FAH-tee „GOO-teh nakht!"

Say "Good Night" to Daddy.

Hast du deine Gebete gesagt?
Hahst doo DIGH-neh geh-BAY-teh geh-ZAHKT?

Did you say your prayers?

Du wirst schwerer!
Doo veerst SHVEHR-ehr!

You're getting heavier!

Mach die Augen zu!
Makh dee AOU-g'n tsoo!

Close your eyes!

110

Leg dich hin!
Lehk dihsh hin!

Lie down!

Sei still!
Zigh shtihl!

Be quiet!

Süsse Träume!
ZEWHS-seh TROY-meh!

Sweet dreams!

Du musst /im Bett bleiben/ schlafen/.
Doo muhst /im bett BLIGH-b'n/ SHLAH-f'n/.

You must /stay in bed/ sleep/.

Du bist noch nicht im Bett?
Doo bihst nokh nihsht im bett?

You're not in bed yet?

Es ist nicht zu früh, zu Bett zu gehen!
Ess ihst nihsht tsoo frewh, tsoo bett tsoo GAY-'n!

It's not too early to go to bed.

Willst du das Licht an?
Vihlst doo dahs lihsht ahn?

Do you want the light on?

Mutti liebt dich!
MUHT-tee leept dihsh!

Mommy loves you!

Bist du nass?
Bihst doo nahs?

Are you wet?

Du zahnst.
Doo tsahnst.

You're teething.

Bist du wach? Schläfst du?
Bihst doo vahsh? Shlehfst doo?

Are you awake? Are you sleeping?

Warum schläfst du noch nicht?
Vah-ROOM shlehfst doo nokh nihsht?

Why aren't you asleep yet?

Du kannst nicht einschlafen?
Doo kahnst nihsht IGHN-shlah-f'n?

You can't fall asleep?

111

Weck /ihn/sie/ nicht auf!
Vehk /een/zee/ nihsht aouf!

Don't awaken/ him/her/!

Was willst du, Kleine?
Vahs vihlst doo, KLIGH-neh?

What do you want,
my little one?

Du hast beim Schlafen dein Gesicht gekratzt.
Doo hahst bighm SHLAH-f'n dighn
geh-ZIKHT geh-KRATST.

You scratched your face
in your sleep.

Ist dir (nicht) wohl?
Ihst deer (nihsht) vohl?

Do you (not) feel well?

Hast du Bauchweh?
Hahst doo BAOUSH-veh?

Do you have a tummy
ache?

Ist es dir schwindlig?
Ihst ess deer SHVIHNT-lish?

Are you dizzy?

Hast du /Kopfschmerzen/Zahnschmerzen/
Fieber/?
Hahst doo / KOHPF-shmehr-ts'n/
TSAHN-shmehr-ts'n/ FEE-buh/?

Do you have a/ headache/
toothache/ fever/?

Es gibt Flecken an deiner Brust. (Windpocken)
Ess ghipt FLEHK-k'n ahn DIGH-nuh brust.
(VIHNT-pah-k'n)

There are spots on your chest.
(Chicken pox)

Die Drüsen sind geschwollen.
Dee DREWH-z'n zihnt geh-SHVOHL-l'n.

Your glands are swollen.

Zeig die Zunge!
Tsighk dee TSOON-geh!

Stick out your tongue!

Du kriegst die Grippe!
Doo kreekst dee GRIHP-peh!

You're getting the flu.

Du hast eine Erkältung.
Doo hahst IGH-neh ehr-KEHL-tung.

You have a cold.

Du /hustest/ niest/.
Doo /HOOS-test/neest/.

You're /coughing/
sneezing/.

Ich messe deine Temperatur.
Ihsh MES-seh DIGH-neh tem-puh-ah-TUHR.

I'll take your temperature.

Du brauchst etwas gegen den Husten.
Doo braoukhst EHT-vahs GAY-g'n dain
HOOS-t'n.

You'll need something
for the cough.

Morgen musst du im Bett bleiben!
MOHR-g'n muhst doo im beht BLIGH-b'n!

Tomorrow you'll have
to stay in bed.

Tut dir /der Arm/der Fuss/ weh?
Toot deer /dehr ahrm/ dehr foos/ veh?

Does your /arm/foot/
hurt?

Willst du ein neues Heftpflaster?
Vihlst doo ighn NOI-ehs HEFT-flahs-tuh?

Do you want a new
bandaid?   *

Hast du gut geschlafen?
Hahst doo goot geh-SHLAH-f'n?

Did you sleep well?

Bist du (noch) müde?
Bihst doo (nokh) MEWH-deh?

Are you (still) tired?

Fühlst du dich besser?
Fewhlst doo dihsh BEHS-suh?

Do you feel better?

Darf ich bei (Name) schlafen?
Dahrf ihsh bigh (Name) SHLAH-f'n?

May I sleep over (name)'s
house?

Darf (Name) bei uns schlafen?
Dahrf (Name) bigh oons SHLAH-f'n?

May (name) sleep over
at our house?

Sag deine Gebete.
Zahk DIGH-neh geh-BAY-teh.

Say your prayers.

Schlaf gut!
Shlahf goot!

Sleep well!

Auf Regen folgt Sonnenschein. After rain comes sunshine.

DAS WETTER   THE WEATHER

"Everybody talks about it." So the saying goes. Now you and your child can talk about it in German! Try sharing a picture book on weather with your child and discuss the pictures using German. This could be more of a "school" kind of chapter if you and your child want to play school. Flash cards to make, maps to draw, temperatures to record, fun to be had!

Es ist schön. Ess ihst sherhn.	It is beautiful.
Was für/ein herrlicher Tag/eine herrliche Nacht/! Vahs fewr /ighn HEHR-likh-uh tahk/ IGH-neh HEHR-lich-eh nakht/!	What a splendid /day/ night/!
Es gibt keine Wolken! Ess ghipt KIGH-neh VOHL-k'n!	There are no clouds.
Es ist /sonnig/ hell/. Ess ihst /ZOHN-nihsh/ hell/.	It is /sunny/ bright/.
Die Sonne scheint. Dee ZOHN-neh shighnt.	The sun's shining.

Heute ist es (sehr) heiss.
HOI-teh ihst ess (zayr) highss.

It's (very) hot today.

Mir ist warm. Es ist Sommer!
Meer ihst vahrm. Ess ihst ZOHM-muh!

I'm warm. It's summer!

Wir haben eine Hitzewelle.
Veer HAH-b'n IGH-neh HIHT-tseh-vel-leh.

We're having a heat wave.

Es gibt kein bisschen Wind. Ich schwitze.
Ess ghipt kighn BIH-syehn vihnt.
Ihsh SHVIT-tseh.

There's not a bit of wind.
I'm sweating.

Es ist /windig/wolkig/.
Ess ihst /VIHN-dihsh/ VOHL-kihsh/.

It's / windy/ cloudy/.

Es ist ein bisschen /kühl/ kalt/.
Ess ihst ighn BIH-syehn /kewhl/ kahlt/.

It's a bit /cool/ cold/.

Du brauchst /eine Jacke/ einen Pulli/.
Doo braoukhst /IGH-neh YAK-keh/
IGH-n'n PULL-lih/.

You need /a jacket/
a pullover/.

Es regnet wie aus Eimern!
Ess RAY-gneht vee aous IGH-mehrn!

It's raining cats and dogs!

Schau /den Regen/den Schnee/ an!
Shaou /dain RAY-g'n/dain shnay /ahn!

Look at /the rain/ the
snow/.

Die Strasse ist voller Pfützen.
Dee SHTRAH-seh ihst FOHL-luh FEWHT-ts'n.

The street is full of
puddles.   *

Zieh dir die Schuhe aus!
Tsee deer dee SHOOH-eh aous!

Take off your shoes!

Deine Schuhe sind nass.
DIGH-neh SHOOH-eh zihnt nahs.

Your shoes are wet.

So ein unangenehmer Tag!
Zoh ighn OON-ahn-geh-nay-meh tahk!

What an unpleasant
day!

So ein scheussliches Wetter!   What awful weather!
Zoh ighn SHOISS-lish-ehs VEHT-tuh!

Es ist schlecht.   It (the weather) is bad.
Ess ihst shlesht.

Es ist (nur) ein Schauer!   It's (only) a shower.
Ess ihst (nuhr) ighn SHAOU-uh!

Es wird /dunkel/ hell/.   It's getting /dark/ light/.
Ess veert /DUHN-kehl/ hell/.

Der Himmel ist /dunkel/ grau/.   The sky is /dark/gray/.
Dehr HIHM-mehl ihst /DUHN-kehl/ graou/.

Es wird bald dunkel.   It will soon be dark.
Ess veert bahlt DUHN-kehl.

Es donnert und blitzt.   It's thundering and
Ess DOHN-nert oont blitst.   lightening.   *

Es hagelt.   It's hailing.
Ess HAH-gehlt.

So ein Sturm!   What a storm!
Zoh ighn shturm!

So ein Nebel! Es ist neblig.   What fog! It's foggy.
Zoh ighn NEH-behl! Ess ihst NEH-blish.

Warte, bis der Regen aufhört.   Wait until the rain stops.
VAHR-teh, bihs dehr RAY-g'n AOUF-hehrt.

Siehst du den Regenbogen?   Do you see the rainbow?
Zeehst doo dain RAY-g'n-boh-g'n?

Es ist echt winterlich (heute)!   It's really wintery
Ess ihst esht VIHN-tuh-lish (HOI-teh)!   (today).

Es fängt an zu schneien!
Ess fenkt ahn tsoo SHNIGH-'n!

It's beginning to snow!

Es schneit!
Ess shnight!

It's snowing.

Es sieht wie /Regen/Schnee/ aus.
Ess zeeht vee /RAY-g'n/ shnay/ aous.

It looks like /rain/ snow/.

Schneeflocken fallen!
SHNAY-flohk-k'n FAL-l'n!

Snowflakes are falling!

Wie der Schnee glitzert!
Vee dehr shnay GLIT-tsert!

How the snow sparkles!

Vielleicht können wir einen Schneemann bauen!
Feel-LIHST KEHRN-n'n veer IGH-n'n
SHNAY-mann BAOU-'n!

Perhaps we can build a
snowman.

Der /Regen/Schnee/ hat aufgehört.
Dehr /RAY-g'n/ shnay/ haht AOUF-geh-hehrt.

The / rain/snow/ has
stopped.

Der Schnee schmilzt.
Dehr shnay shmiltst.

The snow is melting.

Kommt Zeit, kommt Rat. Time will tell.

DIE ZEIT	TIME

Wieviel Uhr ist es?
VEE-feel OO-uh ihst ess?

What time is it?

Es ist ein Uhr.
Ess ihst ighn OO-uh.

It is one o'clock.

Es ist zwei Uhr.
Ess ihst tsvigh OO-uh.

It is two o'clock.

Es ist Viertel nach drei.
Ess ihst FEER-tehl nakh drigh.

It is quarter after three.

Es ist halb zehn.
Ess ihst hahlp tsehn.

It is nine thirty.

Es ist Viertel vor sieben.
Ess ihst FEER-tehl fohr ZEE-b'n.

It is quarter of seven.

Es ist zwanzig nach sechs.
Ess ihst TSVAHN-tsish nakh zex.

It is six twenty.

Es ist zwanzig vor sieben.
Ess ihst TSVAHN-tsish fohr ZEE-b'n.

It is twenty of seven.

Es ist acht Uhr.
Ess ihst ahkt OO-uh.

It is eight o'clock.

Es ist neun Uhr.
Ess ihst noin OO-uh.

It is nine o'clock.

Es ist zehn Uhr zehn.
Ess ihst tsehn OO-uh tsehn.

It is ten after ten o'clock.

Es ist elf Uhr.
Ess ihst elf OO-uh.

It is eleven o'clock.

Es ist zwölf Uhr dreissig.
Ess ihst tsvelf OO-uh DRIGH-sish.

It is twelve thirty.

Es ist / Nacht/ Mitternacht/.
Ess ihst/ nakht/ MIHT-tuh-nakht/.

It is /night/ midnight/.

Es ist Mittag.
Ess ihst MIHT-tahk.

It is noon (midday)

Es ist /Morgen/ Nachmittag/ Abend/.
Ess ihst /MOHR-g'n/ NAKH-miht-tahk/
AH-behnt/.

It is /morning/ afternoon/
evening/.

Es ist /früh/ spät/.
Ess ihst /frewh/ shpeht/.

It is /early/ late/.

Es dauert eine /kurze/ lange/ Zeit.
Ess DAW-ehrt IGH-neh /KUHR-tseh/
LAHN-geh/ tsight.

It lasts a /short/ long/ time.

Möglichst bald. Jetzt!
MEHRK-lishst bahlt.Yehtst!

As soon as possible.
Now!

In der Zukunft.
In dehr TSUH-kuhnft.

In the future.

119

Hülle und Fülle haben ... to have a great abundance

QUANTITÄTEN	QUANTITIES
Wie alt ist /Mutti/ Vati/? Vee ahlt ihst /MUHT-tee/FAH-tee/?	How old is /mommy/ daddy/?
Wie viele Finger siehst du? Vee FEE-leh FIN-guh zeehst doo?	How many fingers do you see?
Wie viele sind es? Vee FEE-leh zihnt ess?	How many are there?
Es ist (bloss) /einer/eine/eins/.(m/f/n) Ess ihst (blohs) /IGH-nuh/ IGH-neh/ ighns/.	There is (only) one.
Es sind (bloss) vier! Ess zihnt (blohs) feer!	There are (only) four.
Ich habe /keinen/keine/keins/. (m/f/n) Ihsh HAH-beh / KIGH-n'n/ KIGH-neh/ kighns/.	I have none.
Es gibt nichts! Ess ghipt nihshts!	There is nothing!

120

Stell es auf den richtigen Platz!
Shtell ess aouf dain RIHSH-tee-g'n plahts!

Place it on the right spot.

Alle Plätzchen sind gegessen!
AHL-leh PLEHTZ-sh'n zihnt geh-GEHS-'n!

All the cookies have
been eaten.

Nach fünfzehn kommt sechzehn.
Nakh FEWNF-ts'n kohmt ZEX-ts'n.

After 15 comes 16.

Zähle von drei bis zehn!
TSEH-leh fonn drigh bihs tsehn!

Count from 3 to 10.

Eins und eins macht zwei.
Ighns oont ighns makht tsvigh.

One and one make two.

Vier minus (weniger) drei ist eins.
Feer MIH-nuhs (VEH-nee-guh) drigh ihst ighns.

Four minus (less) three
is one.

Zwei mal eins macht zwei.
Tsvigh mahl ighns makht tsvigh.

Two times one makes two.

Sechs durch zwei macht drei.
Zex doorkh tsvigh makht drigh.

Six divided by two makes
three.

Zwei, vier, und sechs sind gerade Zahlen.
Tsvigh, feer oont zex zihnt geh-RAH-deh
TSAH-l'n.

Two, four and six are even
numbers.

Drei, fünf und sieben sind ungerade Zahlen.
Drigh, fewfnf oont ZEE-b'n zihnt
OON-geh-rah-deh TSAH-l'n.

Three, five and seven are
uneven numbers.

Zwei Hälften.
Tsvigh HEHLF-t'n.

Two halves.

Die Bruchrechnung: ein halbes, ein Drittel,
ein Viertel, Dreiviertel.
Dee BRUSCH-resch-nung: ighn HAHL-behs,
ighn DRIHT-tehl, ighn FEER-tehl,
DRIGH-feer-tehl.

Fractions: a half, a third,
a fourth, three-fourths.

121

Ein bisschen /weniger/ mehr/.		A little / less/ more/	
Ighn BIH-syehn /VEH-nee-guh/ mayr/.			
/Einige/ein paar/		/Some/ a few/	
/IGHN-ee-geh/ ighn pahr/			
Mehrere		Several	
MEHR-reh-reh			
/Viele/ eine Menge/		/many/ a lot/	
/FEE-leh/ IGH-neh MEN-geh/			

Null (null)	0	vierzehn	14
eins (ighns)	1	fünfzehn	15
zwei (tsvigh)	2	sechzehn	16
drei (drigh)	3	siebzehn	17
vier (feer)	4	achtzehn	18
fünf (fewnf)	5	neunzehn	19
sechs (zex)	6	zwanzig	20
sieben (ZEE-b'n)	7	einundzwanzig	21
acht (ahkt)	8	zweiundzwanzig	22
neun (noin)	9	dreiundzwanzig	23
zehn (tsehn)	10	dreissig	30
elf (elf)	11	einunddreissig	31
zwölf (tsvelf)	12	zweiunddreissig	32
dreizehn	13	dreiunddreissig	33

vierzig	40		neunzig	90
einundvierzig	41		einundneunzig	91
zweiundvierzig	42		zweiundneunzig	92
dreiundvierzig	43		dreiundneunzig	93
fünfzig	50		hundert	100
einundfünfzig	51		hundert eins	101
zweiundfünfzig	52		hundert zwei	102
dreiundfünfzig	53		hundert drei	103
sechzig	60		zweihundert	200
einundsechzig	61		zweihundert eins	201
zweiundsechzig	62		zweihundert zwei	202
dreiundsechzig	63		zweihundert drei	203
siebzig	70		dreihundert	300
einundsiebzig	71		dreihundert eins	301
zweiundsiebzig	72		dreihundert zwei	302
dreiundsiebzig	73		dreihundert drei	303
achtzig	80		vierhundert	400
einundachtzig	81		vierhundert eins	401
zweiundachtzig	82		vierhundert zwei	402
dreiundachtzig	83		vierhundert drei	403

fünfhundert	500	neunhundert	900
fünfhundert eins	501	neunhundert eins	901
fünfhundert zwei	502	neunhundert zwei	902
fünfhundert drei	503	neunhundert drei	903
sechshundert	600	tausend	1000
sechshundert eins	601	zweitausend	2000
sechhundert zwei	602	dreitausend fünfhundert	3500
sech hundert drei	603	zehntausend	10,000
siebenhundert	700	hundert tausend	100,000
siebenhundert eins	701	eine Million	1,000,000
siebenhundert zwei	702	zwei Millionen	2,000,000
siebenhundert drei	703		
achthundert	800		
achthundert eins	801		
achthundert zwei	802		
achthundert drei	803		

Übung macht den Meister.   Practice makes perfect.

DAS ALFABET   ALPHABET

A	B	C	D	E	F	G
ah	bay	tsay	day	ay	ef	gay

H	I	J	K	L	M	N
hah	ee	jot	kah	ell	emm	enn

O	P	Q	R	S	T	U
oh	pay	kooh	err	ess	tay	oo

V	W	X	Y	Z
faou	vay	ix	ipsilon	tsett

Welcher Buchstabe ist das?   What letter is this?
VEHL-cher BOOHK-shtah-beh ihst dahs?

Hier ist der Buchstabe A.   Here is the letter A.
Heer ihst dehr BOOHK-shtah-beh ah.

Sag diesen Buchstaben.   Read this letter.
Zahk DEE-z'n BOOHK-shtah-b'n.

125

Wie viele Buchstaben gibt es im Wort "cat"?
Vee FEE-leh BOOHK-shtah-b'n ghipt ess im
vohrt "kat"?

How many letters are
in the word "cat"?

Wo ist der Buchstabe H?
Voh ihst dehr BOOHK-shtah-beh hah?

Where is the letter H?

Zeig auf den Buchstaben W.
Tsighk aouf dain BOOHK-shtah-b'n vay.

Point to the letter W.

Was bedeutet dieses Wort?
Vahs beh-DOI-teht DEE-zehs vohrt?

What does this word
mean?

Wessen Name ist das?
VEHS-s'n NAH-meh ihst dahs?

Whose name is this?

Halte den Bleistift nicht so fest.
HAHL-teh dain BLIGH-shtift nihsht zoh fehst.

Don't hold the pencil
tightly.

Halte ihn so.
HAHL-teh een zoh.

Hold it like this.

Schreib nach unten und dann nach rechts
für den Buchstaben L.
Shrighp nakh OON-t'n oont dahn nakh rekhts
fewr dain BOOHK-shtah-b'n ell.

Write down and then to
the right for the letter L.

Kannst du schreiben?
Kahnst doo SHRIGH-b'n?

Do you know how to
write?

Ich kann schreiben.
Ihsh kahn SHRIGH-b'n.

I know how to write.

Ich schreibe das Alphabet.
Ihsh SHRIGH-beh dahs AHL-fah-beht.

I'm writing the alphabet.

Ein goldener Schlüssel öffnet alle Tore. A golden key opens every door.

KINDERREIME	NURSERY RHYMES

Nursery rhymes are a marvelous way to soothe a crying baby, fill a few empty minutes, or just enjoy for their own rhythm. Trusting that the reader already knows the English version of these rhymes, we have chosen to translate them more closely to the German text so that, even though stilted at times, the literal translation of the German words will be understood by the reader. (These rhymes have been translated into German by Mark Hobson. These are written as they were recited to his little sons.)

Bäh, bäh, schwarzes Schaf	Baa Baa Black Sheep
Bäh, Bäh schwarzes Schaf,	Baa Baa black sheep,
hast du etwas Woll'	have you any wool?
Ja mein Herr, ja mein Herr, drei Säcke voll	Yes sir, yes sir three bags full.
Einen für den Meister	One for my master,
und einen für die Frau	and one for the dame
Einen für den kleinen Bub,	One for the little boy,
der wohnt auf der Au.	who lives down in the field.

Humpty Dumpty	Humpty Dumpty
Humpty Dumpty sass auf der Lauer,	Humpty Dumpty sat on
Humpty Dumpty fiel von der Mauer.	look out.
	Humpty Dumpty fell from
	the wall.

Drei kleine Katzen

Drei kleine Katzen
verloren ihre Fäustlinge
und fingen an zu weinen.
Ach Mütterlein, wir meinen leider,
unsere Fäustlinge sind weg!

Was, die Fäustlinge verloren,
ihr bösen Katzen,
Dann bekommt ihr doch keinen Kuchen!
miau, miau, miau,
nein, ihr bekommt doch keinen Kuchen!

Kätzchen, Kätzchen, wo warst du denn?
Ich war in London und besuchte die Königin.
Kätzchen, Kätzchen, was hast du dort getan?
Ich habe eine kleine Maus unter ihren
Stuhl verscheucht.

Drei blinde Mäuschen

Drei blinde Mäuschen, drei blinde Mäuschen,
Sieh mal, wie sie laufen,
Sieh mal, wie sie sausen.
Sie laufen gerne der Bäuerin nach,
Sie schneidet ihnen die Schwänze
mit dem Küchenmesser ab
Hast du im Leben schon so 'was gesehen?
Drei blinde Mäuschen.

Diddle, diddle, Knödel

Diddle, diddle, Knödel,
mein Sohn Jan
ging zu Bett mit den Hosen an.
Mit einem Schuh an-, und einem ausgezogen,
Diddle, diddle, Knödel,
mein Sohn Jan mit den Hosen.

Three Little Kittens

Three little kittens
lost their mittens
and they began to cry.
Oh mother dear, unfortunately,
our mittens are gone away!

What! the mittens are lost!
You naughty kittens,
Then you shall have no cake!
meow, meow meow
No, you shall have no cake!

Kittens, kittens, where were you?
I was in London to see the Queen.
Kittens, kittens what have you done?
I have a little frightened a little
under the stool.

Three Blind Mice

Three blind mice, three blind mice,
See how they run,
See how they rush!
They run after the farmer's wife,
She cuts off their tales
with a kitchen knife,
Have you seen such a sight in your life?
The three blind mice.

Diddle , Diddle, Dumpling

Diddle , diddle, dumpling
my son John,
Went to bed with his pants on.
With one shoe on and one shoe off,
Diddle, diddle, dumpling
my son John (with his pants).

Jack, sei flink, Jack, sei schnell

Jack, sei flink, Jack, sei schnell
Jack, spring über die Kerze so hell!

Meege, Meege, Meige Hi diddle diddle

Meege, Meege, Meige,
Die Katze spielt die Geige
Die Kuh springt über den Mond.
Der kleine Hund lacht,
so etwas zu seh'n,
und der Teller läuft weg mit dem Löffel.

Georgie Porgie, Pudding und Torte

Georgie Porgie, Pudding und Torte
küsste die Mädchen und brachte sie zum Weinen.
Und kamen die Jungs zum Spielen heraus,
Nahm Georgie Porgie sofort Reissaus!

Der alte König Cole

Der alte König Cole
war eine lustige Seele,
eine lustige Seele war er.
Er rief nach seiner Pfeife,
er rief nach seiner Schüssel,
er rief nach seinen Geigenspielern drei.

Jäck Pett mag das Essen nicht fett

Jäck Pett mag das Essen nicht fett,
seine Frau mag das Essen nicht mager.
So putzen denn die zwei zu Haus
fein säuberlich die Teller aus.

Jack Be Nimble, Jack Be Quick.

Jack be nimble, Jack be quick,
Jack jump over the candle so bright!

Hey, Diddle, Diddle

Hey, diddle, diddle!
The cat plays the fiddle,
The cow jumps over the moon;
The little dog laughs,
Something to see,
And the dish runs away with the
spoon.

Georgy Porgy

Georgy Porgy, pudding and pie,
Kissed the girls and made them cry.
And when the boys came out to play,
Georgy Porgy at once cleared out!

Old King Cole

Old King Cole
Was a merry old soul,
A merry old soul was he;
He called for his pipe,
He called for his bowl
He called for his fiddlers three!

Jack Sprat

Jack Sprat could eat no fat,
His wife could eat no lean;
And so, between them both,
They licked the platter clean.

Vater Unser

Vater Unser, der du bist im Himmel
Geheiligt werde Dein Name.
Dein Reich komme, Dein Wille geschehe
wie im Himmel also auch auf Erden.
Unser tägliches Brot gib uns heute,
und vergib uns unsere Schulden
wie wir auch unseren Schuldigern vergeben.
Und führe uns nicht in Versuchung,
sondern erlöse uns von dem Bösen.
Amen

Our Father

Our Father, who are in heaven,
hallowed be thy name;
Thy kingdom come, Thy will be done
on earth as it is in heaven.
Give us this day our daily bread;
and forgive us our trespasses
as we forgive those who offend us
And lead us not into temptation,
but deliver us from evil.
Amen

Ein Psalm Davids

Der Herr ist mein Hirte,
mir wird nichts mangeln.
Er weidet mich auf einer grünen Aue
und führet mich zum frischen Wasser.
Er erquicket meine Seele.
Er führet mich auf rechter Strasse um seines
/Namens willen.
Und ob ich schon wanderte im finstern Tal,
fürchte ich kein Unglück;
denn du bist bei mir,
dein Stecken und Stab trösten mich.
Du bereitest vor mir einen Tisch
im Angesicht meiner Feinde.
Du salbest mein Haupt mit Öl
und schenkest mir voll ein.
Gutes und Barmherzigkeit werden mir folgen
mein Leben lang,
und ich werde bleiben im Hause des Herrn
immerdar.

Psalm 23

The Lord is my shepherd,
there is nothing I shall want.
He reposes me in green pastures
and leads me to fresh water.
He refreshes my soul.
He leads me in right ways for the sake
of His name.
Though I wander in the dark valley
I fear no evil;
for you are near me.
Your rod and staff give me courage.
You prepare a table before me
in the sight of my foes;
You anoint my head with oil;
and fill my cup fully.
Goodness and kindness will follow me
my whole life;
And I will dwell in the house of the Lord
forever.

Ein Tischgebet

Mein Gott, für Speis und Trank
Sagen wir dir Lob und Dank.

A Prayer before Meals

My God, for the food and drink
We say to you praise and thanks.

VOCABULARY

die Familie   The Family

die Mutter	mommy	der Sohn	son
der Vater	grandfather	die Schwester	sister
die Tante	aunt	die Frau	woman, wife
der Onkel	daddy	die Tochter	daughter
die Grossmutter	grandmother	der Bruder	brother
der Grossvater	uncle	der Mann	man, husband
die Kusine	cousin (f)	das Mädchen	girl
der Vetter	cousin (m)	der Junge	boy
die Nichte	niece	das Kind	child
der Neffe	nephew	Fräulein	Miss
die Enkelin	granddaughter	Frau	Mrs.
der Enkel	grandson, grandchild	Herr	Mister

Kosenamen   Endearments

meine Süsse	my sweetie	mein Liebling	sweetie
meine Prinzessin	my princess	mein Prinz	my prince
meine Püppchen	my doll	mein Liebchen	darling, sweetheart
meine Kleine	my little girl	mein Schatz	treasure
mein Kleiner	my little boy		

die Farben   Colors

grün	green	blau	blue
schwarz	black	weiss	white
orange	orange	rot	red
gelb	yellow	lila	purple
rosa	pink	braun	brown
grau	grey		

die Wochentage   Days

(am) Montag	(on) Monday	(am) Dienstag	(on) Tuesday
(am) Mittwoch	(on) Wednesday	(am) Donnerstag	(on) Thursday
(am) Freitag	(on) Friday	(am) Samstag	(on) Saturday
(am) Sonntag	(on) Sunday		

die Monate — Months

(im) Januar	(in) January	(im) Februar	(in) February
(im) März	(in) March	(im) April	(in) April
(im) Mai	(in) May	(im) Juni	(in) June
(im) Juli	(in) July	(im) August	(in) August
(im) September	(in) September	(im) Oktober	(in) October
(im) November	(in) November	(im) Dezember	(in) December

die Jahreszeiten — Seasons

(im) Frühling	(in) spring	(im) Sommer	(in) summer
(im) Herbst	(in) fall	(im) Winter	(in) winter

die Feiertage — Holidays

der Geburtstag	birthday	der Vatertag	Father's Day
Neujahrstag	New Year's Day	das Dankfest	Thanksgiving Day
Washingtons Geburtstag	Washington's Birthday	das Fest der Lichter	Hanukkah
Lincolns Geburtstag	Lincoln's Birthday	der Heiligabend	Christmas Eve
Valentinstag	St. Valentine's	das Weihnachten	Christmas
das Ostern	Easter	der Sylvester	New Year's Eve
das Passah	Passover		
der Muttertag	Mother's Day		

das Kinderzimmer — Nursery

die Saugflasche	baby bottle	die Badewanne	bathtub
das Buch	book	der Kinderwagen	carriage
das Kinderbettchen	crib	die Windel	diaper
der Schnuller	pacifier	der Kinderstuhl	high chair
der Schaukelstuhl	rocking chair	der Laufstall	play pen
die Sicherheitsnadel	safety pin	der Sportwagen	stroller
		das Spielzeug	toy

das Spielzeug   Toys

das Flugzeug	airplane	der Klebstoff	paste
der Ball	ball	das Sparschweinchen	piggy
der Luftballon	balloon		bank
der Stock	bat	die Marionette	puppet
die Perle	bead	das Puzzle	puzzle
das Fahrrad	bicycle	der Rechen	rake
die Bauklötze	blocks	die Rassel	rattle
das Boot	boat	der Ring	ring
der Bulldozer	bull dozer	die Rakete	rocket
der Bus	bus	das Schaukelpferd	rocking
das Auto	car		horse
der Kinderwagen	carriage	das Seil	rope
das Schachbrett	chess board	das Segelboot	sailboat
der Ton	clay	der Sandkasten	sand box
der Clown	clown	die Schere	scissors
das Malbuch	coloring book	der Roller	scooter
der Buntstift	crayon	die Wippe	see-saw
die Puppe	doll	der Rollschuh	skate
das Puppenhaus	doll house	das Rollbrett	skateboard
der Drache	dragon	der Schlitten	sled
die Trommel	drum	die Rutschbahn	slide
die Angelrute	fishing rod	der Soldat	soldier
die Festung	fort	das U-Boot	submarine
der Globus	globe	die Schaukel	swing
der Drachenflieger	hang glider	das Schwimmbad	swimming pool
der Hubschrauber	helicopter	der Panzer	tank
das Horn	horn		(military)
der Indianer	Indian	das Teeservice	tea set
das Schachtelmännchen	Jack-in-the-box	der Teddybär	Teddy Bear
das Springseil	jump rope	der Schläger	tennis
der Drachen	kite		racquet
die Murmel	marble	das Zelt	tent
die Maske	mask	der Kreisel	top
der Malkasten	paintbox	die Spielzeugtruhe	toy box
der Pinsel	paint brush	der Traktor	tractor
der Panda	panda	die Eisenbahn	train set
		das Dreirad	tricycle
		der Lastwagen	truck
		der Wagen	wagon
		die Pfeife	whistle

die Kleider   Clothes

der Rucksack	backpack
der Bademantel	bathrobe
der Badeanzug	bathing suit
der Gürtel	belt
das Lätzchen	bib
die Bluse	blouse
der Stiefel	boot
der Mantel	coat
das Kleid	dress
die Brille	glasses
der Handschuh	glove
das Taschentuch	handkerchief
der Hut	hat
die Jacke	jacket
die Jeans	jeans
das Nachthemd	night gown
der Schlafanzug	pajamas
der Anorak	parka
die Handtasche	pocketbook
der Regenmantel	raincoat

die Gummischuhe	rubbers
die Sandale	sandal
das Hemd	shirt
der Schuh	shoe
das Schnürband	shoe lace
die kurze Hose	shorts
die Hosen	slacks
der Pantoffel	slipper
der Turnschuh	sneaker
die Socken	socks
der Sweater	sweater
das T-shirt	T-shirt
die Strumpfhose	tights
der Regenschirm	umbrella
die Unterhose	underpants
das Unterhemd	undershirt
die Unterwäsche	underwear
die Brieftasche	wallet

Unterhaltungsmöglichkeiten   Entertainments

der Vergnügungspark	amusement park
das Aquarium	aquarium
der Baseball	baseball
der Basketball	basketball
der Strand	beach
das Camping	camping
der Zirkus	circus
das Konzert	concert
der Jahrmarkt	fair
das Fischen	fishing
das Spiel	game
die Gymnastik	gymnastics
(das) Wandern	hiking
das Kino	movie theatre
das Museum	museum

die Party	party
der Park	park
das Picknick	picnic
der Spielplatz	playground
das Restaurant	restaurant
(das) Reiten	riding (horseback)
(das) Segeln	sailing
Einkäufe machen	to shop
(das) Eislaufen	skating (ice)
(das) Skifahren	skiing
(das) Fussballspiel	soccer match
der Sport	sports
(das) Schwimmen	swimming
(der) Volleyball	volleyball
zu Fuss gehen	to walk
der Tierpark	zoo

135

der menschliche Körper — Human Body

der Knöchel	ankle	die Hand	hand
der Arm	arm	der Kopf	head
der Rücken	back	die Ferse	heel
der Bauch	belly	die Hüfte	hip
der Nabel	belly button	der Kiefer	jaw
der Popo	bottom	das Knie	knee
die Backe	cheek	das Bein	leg
die Brust	chest	die Lippe	lip
das Kinn	chin	der Mund	mouth
das Ohr	ear	der Hals	neck
der Ellbogen	elbow	die Nase	nose
das Auge	eye	die Schulter	shoulder
die Augenbraue	eyebrow	der Bauch	stomach
das Augenlid	eyelid	die Kehle	throat
das Gesicht	face	der Daumen	thumb
der Finger	finger	die Zehe	toe
der Fingernagel	fingernail	die Zunge	tongue
die Stirn	forehead	die Taille	waist
das Haar	hair	das Handgelenk	wrist

die Getränke — Beverages

das Bier	beer	der Orangensaft	orange juice
der Kakao	cocoa	das Orangengetränk	orange drink
der Kaffee	coffee	die Limo	soda
der Fruchtsaft	fruit juice	der Tee	(a cup of) tea
der Saft	juice	der Tee	Tea with
das Zitronengetränk	lemon drink	mit Zitrone	with lemon
die Milch	milk	das Wasser	water
		der Wein	wine

die Behälter — Containers

der Sack	bag	der Kasten	crate
die Flasche	bottle	der Briefumschlag	envelope
die Schachtel	box, carton	das Gefäss	jar
		der Deckel	top, lid

Nachspeisen / Dessert

der Apfelkuchen	apple cake	der Pfannkuchen	fritter
der Kuchen	cake	das Eis	ice cream
das Bonbon	candy	der Pfannkuchen	pancake
die Schokolade	chocolate	der Pudding	pudding
das Plätzchen	cookie	der Milchreis	rice pudding
die Eiercreme	custard	der Joghurt	yoghurt

Gemüsesorten / Kinds of Vegetables

der Spargel	asparagus	die Zwiebel	onion
die rote Bete	beet	die Petersilie	parsley
die Brokkoli	broccoli	die Erbse	pea
der Rosenkohl	Brussel sprout	der Paprika	pepper (green)
die Karotte	carrot	die Kartoffel	potato
der Blumenkohl	cauliflower	der Kürbis	pumpkin
der Sellerie	celery	das Radieschen	radish
der Mais	corn	der Spinat	spinach
die Gurke	cucumber	die Bohne	stringbean
der Knoblauch	garlic	die Tomate	tomato
der Salat	lettuce	die Rübe	turnip
der Pilz	mushroom		

Fleischsorten / Kinds of Meat

der Speck	bacon	der Hamburger	hamburger
das Hühnchen	chicken	die Wurst	sausage
das Kotelett	chop	das Steak	steak
der Schinken	ham	der Truthahn	turkey

Meeresfrüchte / Seafood

der Karpfen	carp	die Sardine	sardine
der Kabeljau	cod	die Garnele	shrimp
der Hering	herring	die Seezunge	sole
der Hummer	lobster	der Schwertfisch	sword fish
der Salm	salmon	die Forelle	trout
		der Thunfisch	tuna

das Obst

Fruit

der Apfel	apple	die Melone	melon
die Aprikose	apricot	die Orange	orange
die Banane	banana	der Pfirsich	peach
die Beere	berry	die Birne	pear
die Blaubeere	bluberry	die Ananas	pineapple
die Kirsche	cherry	die Pflaume	plum
die Kokosnuss	coconut	die Rosine	raisin
die Weintraube	grape	die Himbeere	raspberry
die Grapefruit	grapefruit	die Erdbeere	strawberry
die Zitrone	lemon	die Mandarine	tangerine

andere Lebensmittel

Other Foods

das Brot	bread	der Pfannkuchen	pancake
das Brötchen	bun, roll	die Erdnuss	peanut
die Butter	butter	die Erdnuss-	peanut
ein Butterbrot	buttered bread	butter	butter
die Cornflakes	cereal	der Pfeffer	pepper (black)
der Kaugummi	chewing gum	die saure Gurke	pickle
die Zuckerwatte	cotton candy		das Popkorn
	popcorn		
der Kräcker	cracker	die Kartoffelchips	potato chips
die Sahne	cream	der Reis	rice
das Spiegelei	egg (fried)	der Salat	salad
die Pommes	French fries	das Salz	salt
Frites		ein belegtes Brot	an open sandwich
die Sosse	gravy	ein Käsebrot	an (open) cheese
der Honig	honey		sandwich
die Marmelade	jam	ein Schinkenbrot	an (open) ham
die Marmelade	jelly		sandwich
der Ketchup	ketchup	die Sosse	sauce
die Marmelade	marmelade	das Sauerkraut	sauerkraut
der Kartoffelbrei	mashed potatoes	die Spaghetti	spaghetti
das Omelett	omelette	der Eintopf	stew
die Nudeln	noodles	der Zucker	sugar
		der Sirup	syrup
		der Toast	toast
		der Weinessig	vinegar

138

Geschirr und Besteck — Dishes and Utensils

die Schüssel	bowl	der Krug	pitcher
die Tasse	cup	der Teller	plate
der Dessertteller	dessert plate	der Topf	pot
das Geschirr	dishes	die Untertasse	saucer
die Gabel	fork	der Suppenteller	soup plate
die Bratpfanne	frying pan	der Löffel	spoon
das Glas	glass	die Tischdecke	tablecloth
der Wasserkessel	kettle	der Esslöffel	tablespoon
das Messer	knife	der Teelöffel	teaspoon
die Serviette	napkin	das Tablett	tray

das Haus — House

der Dachboden	attic	der Blumengarten	flower garden
die Hintertür	back door	die Garage	garage
der Hof	back yard	der Mülleimer	garbage pail
der Keller	basement	das Tor	gate
das Badezimmer	bathroom	das Gras	grass
das Schlafzimmer	bedroom	die Hecke	hedge
die Bank	bench	der Schlauch	hose
der Busch	bush	die Küche	kitchen
die Decke	ceiling	der Rasensprenger	lawn sprinkler
der Kamin	chimney	das Wohnzimmer	living room
der Schrank(Kleide)	closet (clothes)	der Briefkasten	mailbox
die Veranda	deck	das Dach	roof
das Esszimmer	dining room	die Treppe	stairs
die Tür	door	der Baum	tree
die Einfahrt	driveway	der Gemüsegarten	vegetable garden
die Steckdose	electric outlet		
der Zaun	fence	die Wand	wall
der Fussboden	floor	das Fenster	window
		der Garten	yard

Wohnmöglichkeiten — Dwellings

die Wohnung	apartment	das Bauernhaus	farm house
die Hütte	cabin	das Hotel	hotel
die Burg	castle	das Wohnmobil	motor home
die Eigentumswohnung	condo	der Palast	palace
das Sommerhaus	cottage	das Zelt	tent
das Landhaus	country house	der Wohnwagen	trailer

139

die Küche   Kitchen

die Schürze	apron	der Mikrowellen-	micro
der Besen	broom	ofen	
der Eimer	bucket	der Mop	mop
der Hängeschrank	cabinet	der Backofen	oven
die Uhr .	clock	der Topf	pot
der Trockner	clothes dryer	der Kühlschrank	refriger
die Waschmaschine	clothes washer		ator
der Computer	computer	die Scheuerbürste	scrub brush
die Arbeitsfläsche	counter	die Nähmaschine	sewing
das Pult	desk		machine
das Waschmittel	detergent	das Spülbecken	sink
das Spültuch	dish cloth	der Schwamm	sponge
die Spülmaschine	dishwasher	der Hocker	stool
die Schublade	drawer	der Herd	stove
das Staubtuch	dust cloth	das Sieb	strainer
der Mixer	electric mixer	der Tisch	table
der Trichter	funnel	der Toaster	toaster
das Bügeleisen	iron	der Staubsauger	vacuum
das Bügelbrett	ironing board		cleaner

das Badezimmer   Bathroom

das Aspirin	aspirin	das Rasiermesser	razor
die Badewanne	bathtub	die Waage	scale
der Fön	blow dryer	das Shampoo	shampoo
die Blase	bubble	die Dusche	shower
der Wasserhahn	faucet	das Waschbecken	sink
der Lippenstift	lipstick	die Seife	soap
die Hausapotheke	medicine cabinet	der Schwamm	sponge
das Mundwasser	mouth wash	das Toilettenpapier	tissue
der Nagellack	nail polish	die Toilette	toilet
das Parfüm	perfume	die Zahnbürste	toothbrush
der Puder	powder	die Zahnpasta	toothpaste
		das Handtuch	towel

das Schlafzimmer — Bedroom

der Wecker	alarm clock	die Lampe	lamp
das Bett	bed	der Spiegel	mirror
die Bettdecke	bedspread	der Nachttisch	night table
die Decke	blanket	das Foto	photograph
die Jalousien	blinds	das Kopfkissen	pillow
der Teppich	carpet	das Plakat	poster
der Kleiderschrank	clothes closet	der Schaukelstuhl	rocking chair
die Daunendecke	comforter	das Schaukelpferd	rocking horse
die Vorhänge	curtains	das Bettlaken	sheet
die Kommode	dresser	das Telefon	telephone
der Kleiderbügel	hanger	der Vorleger	throw rug

das Wohnzimmer — Living Room

die Klimaanlage	air conditioner	der Heizkörper	heater
der Sessel	arm chair	das Klavier	piano
das Bücherregal	book case	das Radio	radio
der Kassetten-rekorder	cassette player	das Regal	shelf
die Kassette	cassette tape	der Fernseher	TV
die CD	compact disk	der Videorekorder	VCR
der Kamin	fireplace		

die Werkzeuge — Tools

der Bohrer	drill	das Sandpapier	sandpaper
der Hammer	hammer	die Säge	saw
die Hacke	hoe	die Schere	scissors
die Leiter	ladder	die Schraube	screw
der Rasenmäher	lawn mower	der Schraubenzieher	screw driver
der Nagel	nail	die Schaufel	shovel
die Nuss	nut	die Kelle	trowel
die Mistgabel	pitchfork	der Schraubstock	vise
die Zange	pliers	der Schubkarren	wheel barrow
der Rechen	rake	der Schrauben-schlüssel	wrench

das Auto — Car

der Rücksitz	back seat	der Sitz	seat
die Batterie	battery	der Sitzgurt	seat belt
das Armaturenbrett	dashboard	das Lenkrad	steering wheel
die Tür	door		
der Türgriff	door handle	der Reifen	tire
der Scheinwerfer	headlight	das Rad	wheel
die Hupe	horn		
der Motor	motor		

Unterwegs — Along the Road

der Flughafen	airport	der Parkplatz	parking lot
die Wohnung	apartment	das Pflaster	pavement
die Panne	break down	der Mast	pole
die Brücke	bridge	die Toilette	rest rooms
das Gebäude	building	der Fluss	river
der Bus	bus	die Schule	school
die Haltestelle	bus stop	der Bürgersteig	sidewalk
das Auto	car	der Wegweiser	sign post
die Autowäsche	car wash	das Tempolimit	speed limit
die Kirche	church	der Sportwagen	sports car
die Ecke	corner	das Stoppschild	stop sign
die Zebrastreifen	crossing	die Strasse	street
der Randstein	curb	die Strassenlaterne	street light
die Fabrik	factory	der Supermarkt	supermarket
der Bauernhof	farm	das Taxi	taxi
das Feld	field	die Telefonzelle	telephone box
die Feuerwache	fire station	der Verkehr	traffic
das Feuerwehrauto	fire truck	der Vehrkehrsstau	traffic jam
die Zapfsäule	gas pump	die Ampel	traffic light
die Tankstelle	gas station	der Zug	train
der Hafen	harbor	der Bahnhof	train station
die Strassenbahn	trolley	der Tankwagen	truck (oil)
die Autobahn	highway	der Abschleppwagen	truck (tow)
das Loch	hole	der Tunnel	tunnel
das Krankenhaus	hospital	der Lieferwagen	van
das Motorrad	motorcycle		
parken	to park		

die Geschäfte   Shops

die Bäckerei	bakery	die Apotheke	drug store
die Bank	bank	das Möbelgeschäft	furniture shop
der Frisör	barber shop	das Lebenmittelgeschäft	grocery store
der Damenfrisör	beauty shop	der Juwelier	jewelry store
die Buchhandlung	book store	der Wäscherei	laundromat
die Reinigung	cleaners	der Holzplatz	lumber yard
das Modegeschäft	clothing store	die Gärtenerei	nursery
das Kaufhaus	department store	das Schuhgeschäft	shoe store
		die Spielwarenladen	toy store

die Berufe   Occupations

der Schauspieler	actor	der Bibliothekar	librarian
die Künstlerin	artist	der Briefträger	mailman
der Astronaut	astronaut	der Mechaniker	mecanic
der Sportler	athlete	der Kaufmann	merchant
der Bäcker	baker	der Geistliche	minister
die Busfahrerin	bus driver	die Krankenschwester	nurse
der Metzger	butcher	der Anstreicher	painter
der Zimmermann	carpenter	die Apothekerin	pharmacist
der Chauffeur	chauffeur	der Pilot	pilot
der Küchenchef	chef	der Polizist	policeman
die Computerprogram-miererin	computer programmer	der Priester	priest
der Koch	cook	der Rennfahrer	race driver
der Cowboy	cowboy	der Matrose	sailor
der Zahnarzt	dentist	der Verkäufer	salesman
der Arzt	doctor	die Verkäuferin	saleswoman
der Ingenieur	engineer	der Taxifahrer	taxi driver
der Bauer	farmer	die Lehrerin (f)	teacher
der Feuerwehrmann	fireman	der Lehrer (m)	teacher
der Fischer	fisherman	der Lokomotivführer	train engineer
der Müllmann	garbage man	der Kellner	waiter
die Gärtnerin	gardener	die Kellnerin	waitress
die Friseuse	hairstylist	der Tierpfleger	zoo keeper
der Rechtsanwalt	lawyer		

143

die Tiere   Animals

der Bär	bear	der Löwe	lion
der Bulle	bull	das Lama	llama
das Kamel	camel	der Maulwurf	mole
die Katze	cat	der Affe	monkey
das Hühnchen	chick	die Maus	mouse
die Kuh	cow	der Ochse	ox
das Krokodil	crocodile	der Panda	panda
das Reh	deer	das Schwein	pig
der Hund	dog	das Ferkel	piglet
der Esel	donkey	das Pony	pony
der Elefant	elephant	das Hündchen	puppy
das Kitz	fawn	der Hase	rabbit
der Fuchs	fox	der Waschbär	raccoon
der Frosch	frog	die Ratte	rat
die Giraffe	giraffe	das Renntier	reindeer
die Ziege	goat	der Hahn	rooster
der Gorilla	gorilla	der Seehund	seal
das Meerschweinchen	guinea pig	die Schlange	snake
der Hamster	hamster	das Eichhörnchen	squirrel
das Flusspferd	hippopotamus	der Tiger	tiger
der Jaguar	jaguar	die Schildkröte	turtle
das Pferd	horse	der Wal	whale
das Känguruh	kangaroo	der Wolf	wolf
das Kätzchen	kitten	der Wurm	worm
das Lamm	lamb		(earth)
der Leopard	leopard	das Zebra	zebra

die Vögel   Birds

der Kanarienvogel	canary	die Eule	owl
das Hühnchen	chicken	der Papagei	parrot
die Ente	duck	der Pelikan	pelican
das Entchen	duckling	die Taube	pigeon
der Adler	eagle	das Rotkehlchen	robin
der Flamingo	flamingo	die Seemöwe	seagull
die Gans	goose	der Spatz	sparrow
das Gänslein	gosling	der Schwan	swan
die Henne	hen	der Truthahn	turkey

die Insekte — Insects

die Ameise	ant	die Heuschrecke	grasshopper
die Biene	bee	der Marienkäfer	lady bug
der Schmetterling	butterfly	die Stechmücke	mosquito
die Raupe	caterpillar	die Motte	moth
die Schabe	cockroach	die Gottesanbeterin	praying mantis
die Grille	cricket	die Spinne	spider
der Floh	flea	die Wespe	wasp
die Fliege	fly		

die Bäume — Trees

der Apfelbaum	apple tree	der Birnbaum	pear tree
der Kirschbaum	cherry tree	die Kiefer	pine
der Christbaum	Christmas tree	die Fichte	spruce
der Ahornbaum	maple tree	die Weide	willow

die Blumen — Flowers

die Azalee	azalea	das Maiglöckchen	lily of the valley
die Butterblume	buttercup		
die Nelke	carnation	die Mimose	mimosa
die Chrysantheme	chrysanthemum	die Orchidee	orchid
die Klematis	clematis	das Stiefmütterchen	pansy
der Krokus	crocus	die Pfingstrose	peony
die gelbe Narzisse	daffodil	die Petunie	petunia
der Löwenzahn	dandelion	das Rhododendron	rhododendron
die Gardenie	gardenia	die Rose	rose
die Geraniel	geranium	die Tulpe	tulip
die Iris	iris	das Veilchen	violet

PRONUNCIATION GUIDE

The following information is provided to answer basic questions which may arise regarding correct German pronunciation. This guide should be considered an approximation. It is difficult to express precisely spoken sounds in written symbols. The pronunciation in the text is, likewise, an approximation.

VOWELS

A: (short) as in *pond.* Example: Mann;
   (long) as in *father.* Example: Vati.
   (ä -long) as in *pail.* Example: schärfen
   (ä-short) as in *men.* Example: Äpfel

E: (short) as in *bed.* Example: Essen;
   (long) as in *day.* Example: Weg
   (unaccented) as in *ago.* Example: Bitte

I: (short) as in *it.* Example: Wind:
   (long) as in *feet.* Example: Hier

O: (short) as in *song.* Example:
   (long) as in *foe.* Example: Boot
   (ö- long) as in *early.* Example: hören
   (ö-short) as in *girl.* Example: Köchin

U: (short) as in *full.* Example: du
   (long) as in *broom.* Example: ruhen
   (ü -long) as in *feel.* Example: für
   (ü -short) as in *pin.* Example: Küsschen

Y: same as ü. Example: typ

COMBINATIONS

AU: as in *mouse.* Example: Maus
EI, AI: as in *sight.* Example: mein
EU, ÄU: as in *toy.* Example: neun

CONSONANTS

B: *b* as in the word *boy*. Example: beben
    p (at the end of a word) as in *map*. Example: gieb

C: *ts* as in *sits*. Example:_____
    k as in *cold*. Example: _____

CH: *kh* as in *huge*. Example: durch

CHS: *k* as in *socks*. Example: wachsen

D: *d* as in *dog* Example: Bruder
    t (at the end of a word) as in *cat*. Example: Hund

G: *g* as in *good*.. Example: tragen
    k as in *back*. Example: tag

H: *h* as in *hurt*. Example: Hand

IG: *ich* in North German Pronunciation. Example: schmutzig

J: *y* as in *yes*. Example: ja

QU: *kv* . Example: Quantitäten

R: (rolled in the throat as in French or trilled at the tip of the tongue as in Spanish.)
    Example: rot

S: *z* as in *is*. Example: lesen.
    sh as in *should*. Example: spielen
    s as in *sing*. Example: das

SS: *s* as in *silly*. Example: Fuss

SCH: *sh* as in *show*. Example: Fleisch

TI, TZ: *ts* as in *sits*. Example: Katze

V: *f* as in *father*. Example: Vati

W: *v* as in *visit*. Example: wir

Z: *ts* as in *sits*. Example: Zeit

147

INDEX

(Blanks are provided on each page for additional vocabulary.)

A		B	
(to be) able	können 14,34,44,57,74	baby	das Baby 36
ache	das weh 112	back	der Rücken 19
adjusted	eingestellt 93,97	backwards	rückwärts 80,90
(to be) afraid	haben Angst 37,103	bacon	der Speck 26
after	nach 18, 57	bad	schlecht 116
again	nochmals 16	bag	die Tasche 73
air mattress	die Luftmatratze 96	to bake	backen 56,63
aisle	der Gang 73	bakery	die Bäckerei 69
bait	der Köder 94	baking powder	das Backpulver 56
airplane	das Flugzeug 75	balance	die Bilanz 78
to be all right	schon gut sein 47	ball	der Ball 35,38,
allowance	das Taschengeld 58		78,88
All aboard!	Geh en Bord! 80	balloon	der Luftballon 87,107
All aboard!	Alles einsteigen! 90	banana	die Banane 27
to be allowed,	dürfen 23,26,44,49, 51,	bandaid	das Heftpflaster 113
may	53,63,75,93,96,113	to bang	schlagen 36
also	auch 61	bank	die Bank 69
animal	das Tier 85,86	barbeque	der Grill 43
another	anderes 45	barefoot	barfuss 51
anyone	jemand 64	to bark	bellen 86
apple	der Apfel 27	bat	der Stock 78
appointment	der Termin 93	bath	das Bad 19
arm	der Arm 33,38,113	bathroom	das Badezimmer
around	um 88		17,20,21,48
to ask	fragen 44,50,75	bathtub	die Wanne 20
(to be) asleep	schlafen 111	battery	die Batterie 83
attic	der Dachboden 95		
awake	wach 111,112		
awful	schrecklich 102		
awful	scheusslich 116		

153

leg	das Bein 86	loud	laut 36
lesson	die Aufgabe 64	to love	lieben 66,111
to let	lassen 28	to lower(boat)	aussetzen 81
Let go!	Lass aus! 32,38	to lower	leiser stellen 51
Let me ...	Lass mich... 28	(volume)	
Let's go	gehen wir 92,98	luck	das Glück 102
letter	der Buchstabe 125	to be lucky	Glück haben 102
library	die Bibliothek 93	lumber yard	der Holzplatz 68
license	der Führerschein 91	lunch	das Mittagessen 25,44,56
to lie down	hinlegen 45, 96,111		
life boat	das Rettungsboot 81		M
to lift	heben 88		
light	das Licht 20,49,111	magazine	die Zeitschrift 83
to lightning	blitzen 116	to make, do	machen 55,56,121
to like	gern haben 37,71	mall	das Einkaufszen-
(something)			trum 70,92
to like (to be	mögen 28,106	Man over-	Mann über Bord !
pleasing to)		board!	81
like this	so 83,84,126	many	viele 122
list	die Liste 68	marble (toy)	die Murmel 87
to listen	zuhören 32, 46,94	Marvelous !	Wunderbar ! 102
little	klein 26	may	dürfen 23,26,27,44,49,
a little	ein bisschen 28		51,53,63,75,83,92,113
to live	wohnen 16	to mean	meinen 105
living room	das Wohnzimmer 49	to measure	messen 113
to load	laden 91	(to take)	
to lock	abschliessen 41	meat	das Fleisch 28
long	lang 34	to meet	treffen 73, 95
look, appear	aussehen 24, 117	to melt	schmelzen 117
to look at	anschauen 32, 34,35,36,43,	merry-go-	das Karussell 87
	90,104,115	round	
to look for	suchen 23, 73	mess	das Durcheinander
loose	weit 72		103
(clothing)		milk	die Milch 28,29
to lose	verlieren 80		
a lot	eine Menge 122		
a lot	viel 64,99		

U

V

W

COLOR, CUT and PASTE

A colorful, fun and easy way to get acquainted with this book is to match the pictures on the next few pages with the sentences in the text. The page number on the back of each drawing is given to help you spot the page you are looking for. An asterisk next to the appropriate sentence is also given to help you pinpoint the exact sentence. Sometimes a picture will match more than one sentence.

German Bingo –

These pages can be used to play German Bingo reenforcing your German vocabulary or, of course, just for fun.

Look on pages 13 – 28 and match
these pictures with the correct sentences.

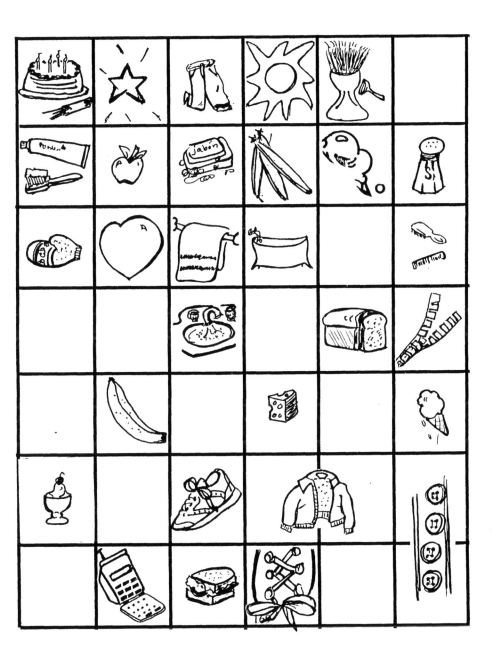

	21	16	23	15	15
27	19	28	20	27	18
24		19	20	14	23
23	29		18		
27		28		27	
		23	22		28
23					
		23	26	13	

Look on pages 29 – 51 and match
these pictures with the correct sentences.

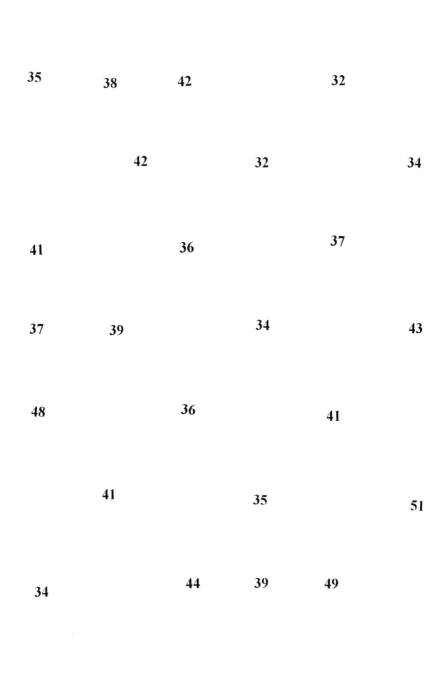

Look on pages 52 - 81 and match
these pictures with the correct sentences.

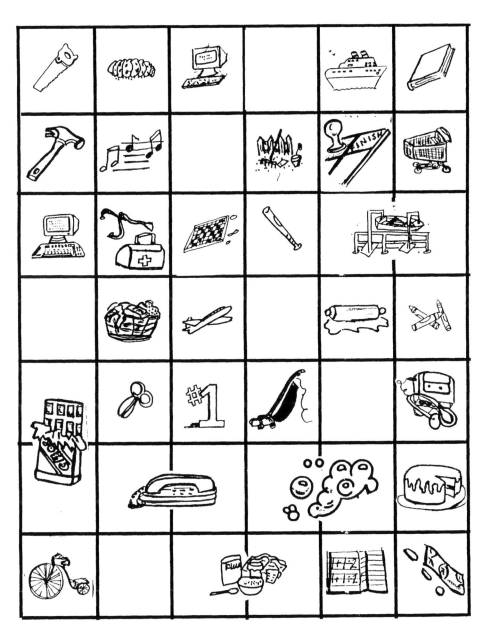

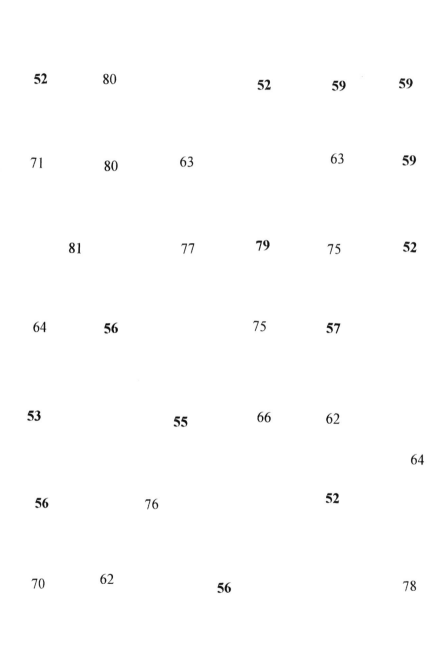

Look on pages 81 – 116 and match
these pictures with the correct sentences.

86 94 86 96 86

82 88 115 96 94 85

95 83 93 83

102 108 81 87 110

89 **87** 91 97

113

89 86 107 110

97 116 95 81 83